Only 20 lucky people a day are allowed to visit **the Wave** in Vermilion Cliffs National Monument in Arizona, U.S.A.

NATIONAL GEOGRAPHIC
KiDS

Bet You Didn't Know!

2

Outrageous, Awesome, Out-of-This-World Facts

NATIONAL GEOGRAPHIC
WASHINGTON, D.C.

Contents

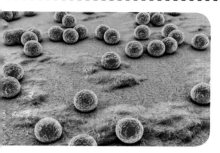

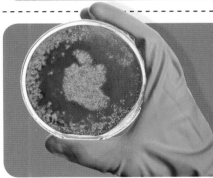

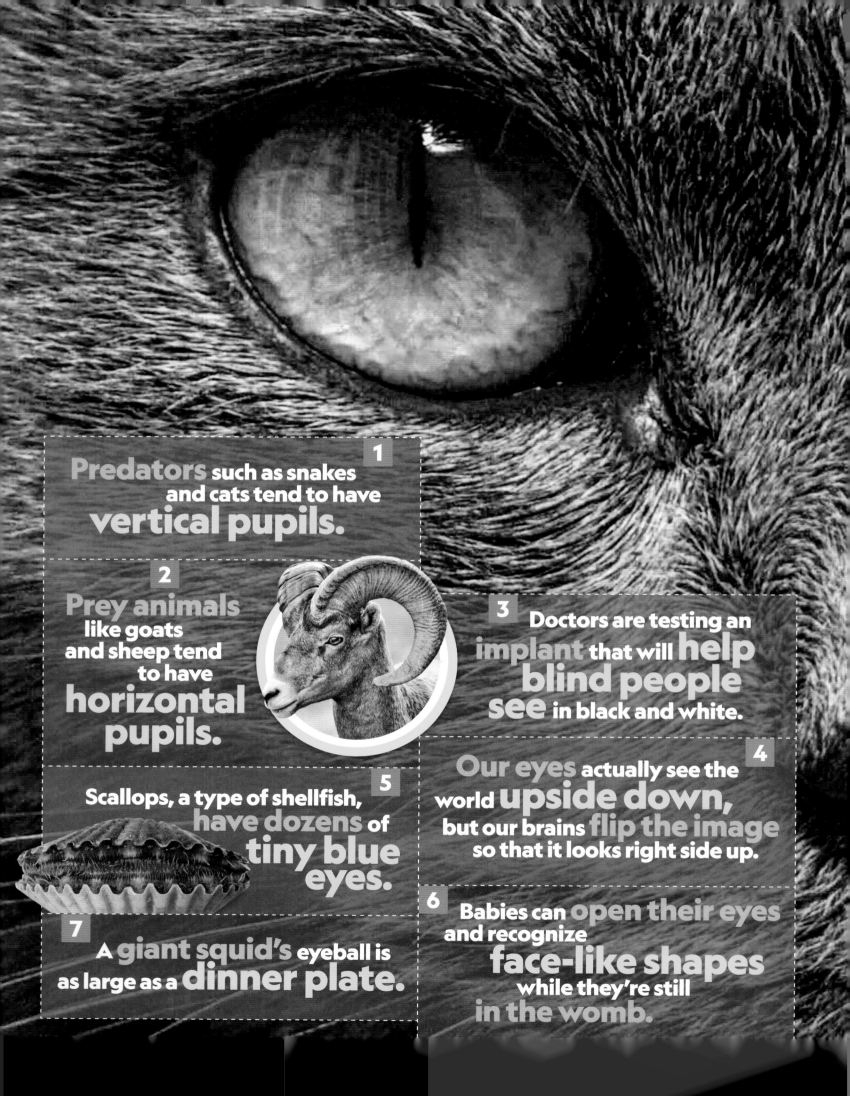

1 Predators such as snakes and cats tend to have **vertical pupils.**

2 Prey animals like goats and sheep tend to have **horizontal pupils.**

3 Doctors are testing an **implant** that will **help blind people see** in black and white.

4 Our eyes actually see the world **upside down,** but our brains **flip the image** so that it looks right side up.

5 Scallops, a type of shellfish, **have dozens** of **tiny blue eyes.**

6 Babies can **open their eyes** and recognize **face-like shapes** while they're still in the womb.

7 A **giant squid's** eyeball is as large as a **dinner plate.**

Eye-Popping
Facts About
Eyes

8 Some people are born with **special retinas** in their eyes that allow them to see **millions** of **extra colors.**

9 Looking at the **large eyes** of some baby animals can produce **chemicals** in your brain that **boost happiness.**

10 When **we stare** at something, our eyes actually move **back and forth** a tiny bit to keep the object **in focus.**

Fabulous Facts

About

Fashion

1 In **Ancient Rome,** only emperors and high-ranking officials could **wear purple.**

2 **Necklaces and rings made from human hair** were once popular fashion items in the United States and Europe.

WHITE ARSENIC, U.S.P.
POISON

3 The poison **arsenic** was once used to **dye fabrics green.**

4 Models wear clothes **made from chocolate** at the **Salon du Chocolat** **fashion show** in **Paris, France.**

8

Worldwide, **people spend** an estimated **$1.2 trillion** each year on **fashion products.**

5

During **Marie Antoinette's** reign, women at the royal court were asked not to wear the **same outfit** twice.

6

7

Since **astronauts can't do laundry in space,** NASA scientists are testing the use of special **exercise clothes** that won't **get smelly** with wear.

8

A study showed that **students who wear a Superman T-shirt** during their exams may get **better scores.**

9

People once **wore live lizards** as **brooches and hair accessories.**

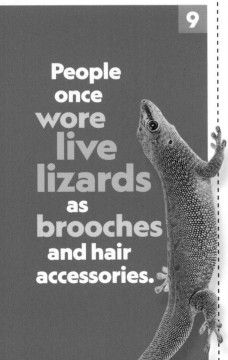

10

The world's **longest wedding dress** stretched for **more than five miles.** (8 km)

9

Wild Facts About Waves

1

The sound of **waves crashing** comes mostly from **air bubbles** in the water.

2

A **surfer** set a **world record** by riding a wave near Portugal that was as tall as a **seven-story building.**

4

Depending on the temperature and conditions, **sound waves** travel about **five times faster in water** than they do **in air.**

people make around a sports stadium, giant **honeybees** use a wave called shimmering to **scare away** hornets.

5

Doldrums are areas of ocean where there is sometimes **no wind or waves.**

6

When you are **thinking creatively,** your brain uses electrical signals called **theta waves.**

7

The **biggest tsunami** ever recorded was **1,720 feet** (524 m) **high,** which is taller than the **Empire State Building!**

8

There's a **deep layer** of cold water called the SOFAR channel that can **carry sound waves** for **thousands of miles—** even across entire oceans!

9

Satellites use **radio waves—** the same waves used to listen to a **car radio—** to communicate with scientists **back on Earth.**

10

Scientists can figure out what types of metals are deep **inside our planet** by studying earthquake **shock waves.**

Toothy

Facts to Bite Into

1 **Llamas** have multiple sets of **sharp fangs** known as **"fighting teeth."**

2 **Small sea snails** called limpets have **teeth stronger than titanium.**

3 **An extinct shark** called *Helicoprion* had **teeth that rotated like a chain saw.**

4 Most **Americans** are familiar with the **Tooth Fairy,** but it's common for children in other parts of the world to **leave their baby teeth** out for a **mouse.**

5 **Before toothbrushes,** people used **"chew sticks"** to clean their teeth.

6 The **first toothbrush,** invented in China in 1498, used **boar bristles** to clean teeth. Toothbrushes with nylon bristles **weren't invented until 1938.**

7 Humans **can bite** with a force of up to **200 pounds** (91 kg).

8 **Crocodiles** bite down with **more force** than **any other living creature:** 3,700 pounds (1,680 kg), which is a little more than the weight of a **medium-size car.**

9 **Tooth enamel** is the **hardest substance** in the human body.

10 **Cows,** goats, and sheep **have no top front teeth.**

What's the Difference?

SEA SNAKE VS. EEL

While both sea snakes and eels stalk the sea for snacks, sea snakes and eels are very different animals. Eels are found in both salt water and freshwater and are actually a species of fish, with fins and gills. Sea snakes, on the other hand, are water-dwelling reptiles that breathe air. Their bodies are shaped just like land snakes', and some species can spend several days at a time on land. Despite their differences, one thing's for sure: Both of these creatures can be dangerous. Sea snakes have some of the most toxic venom around. Eels, on the other hand, defend themselves with vicious teeth, and if it's an electric species, they can even give you a strong zap. If you find one of these wiggly beasts in the water or an aquarium, leave it be and watch it (from a safe distance) slither through its underwater world.

FRECKLES VS. MOLES

Skin freckles and moles are a normal part of human skin, but some cultures have treated the spots just like hairstyles or anything else we wear. In the late 18th century, French aristocrats added fake beauty marks to their faces. The truth is that freckles and moles have nothing to do with fashion. Freckles develop when fair-skinned people spend a lot of time in the sun. The sun produces ultraviolet light, and when some people are exposed to it at a young age, skin cells on their bodies called melanocytes produce a pigment called melanin in small, uneven blotches that we call freckles. Meanwhile, moles are an overgrowth of melanocytes that form a little bump or flat circle, which some people are born with. The shape of our freckles and moles can't be changed at will. But whether you've got spots or not, your skin can be damaged by the sun, so make sure to put on sunscreen before you hit the beach!

MARSHMALLOW VS. MERINGUE

How can you tell these two sugary-sweet substances apart? Early marshmallows were made with the marsh-dwelling mallow plant. The first modern version of the sweet showed up in 19th-century France, where sugar and egg whites were added to the plant's roots to create cough syrup or gummy vitamins. In the 1800s, production spread to the United States, where the plant extract was swapped out for a spongy protein called gelatin. The marshmallow changed once more in the 1950s, when a manufacturer pumped it up with air to make the squishy texture we love today. Meringue, however, is egg whites whipped with sugar into a fluffy topping or baked into a crunchy shell. Bon appétit!

SNAIL VS. SLUG

Hungry birds might be happy to see either of these slimy specimens in a garden, but the average gardener probably won't be pleased! Snails and slugs both have squishy bodies and leave a trail of slime wherever they go. They're both gastropods, a name that translates to "stomach foot." But these two creatures are not quite the same. Snails eat rocks and shells to ooze enough calcium carbonate to form an elaborate spiral shell that they can use for shelter and protection. While snails can retreat into their shells to stay moist, slugs have to head underground or beneath plants and trees to keep from drying out. Shell or no shell, these critters both devour just about everything in their path, but it takes them some time to chow down on budding plants and veggies. Far from speedy, slugs and snails travel at about .029 miles an hour (.0467 km/h). Now that's what you call a snail's pace!

TOMATO VS. TOMATILLO

Their names sound alike. You can make salsa out of both. And a tomatillo looks just like a tiny green tomato. So, are they the same? Turns out, the answer is no. Unlike tomatoes, tomatillos taste more tart and grow inside a papery husk that must be peeled away before they can be eaten. Tomatoes and tomatillos may be distant cousins of one another, but tomatillos are actually more closely related to gooseberries and ground cherries. The two plants are part of the deadly nightshade family, along with potatoes, peppers, and eggplants. Like all nightshades, the leaves and stems of the plants are poisonous. So, if you're trying to decide between tomatoes or tomatillos for your salsa recipe, whichever way you go, just stick with the fruit!

COMET VS. METEOR VS. METEORITE

You're stargazing and you see a bright streak in the night sky. It could be a meteor, also known as a shooting star, or it could be a comet. So, how do you know what to call it? Scientists often call comets "dirty snowballs" because they're made up of ice with bits of dirt, mud, and rocks held together in a tight ball. Comets also contain a blend of gases, including carbon dioxide, ammonia, and methane. When they streak across the solar system, the ice in the comet heats up and releases the gas and dust to form a long tail, which stargazers can sometimes see for several nights without a telescope. While comets put on a long show, meteors only make a quick stop and burn bright. Meteors come from meteoroids, which are small chunks from comets or other rocky objects in space. When meteoroids fly into Earth's atmosphere, they burn up as meteors, which is why you'd only spot them for a few seconds. To make things more confusing, if a piece of the meteor makes it through the atmosphere and lands on the surface, that's called a meteorite. So, if you're looking for a quick way to tell them apart, remember that comets are ice-cool and meteors rock.

Comet

Freaky Facts About Fungi

1 Truffle-sniffing **pigs** can find the **expensive mushrooms** even when they're growing **three feet** (1m) **underground.**

2 The **largest living thing** in the world is a network of **honey mushrooms** that's about **three times** as big as New York City's **Central Park.**

3 **Earth** was once **covered** in giant, **tree-size** mushrooms.

4 Some mushrooms use an **enzyme called luciferase** to **glow in the dark** the same way **fireflies do.**

5

Fungi are **more closely related to animals** than they are to **plants.**

6

Scientists are using some mushrooms to **develop new medicines.**

7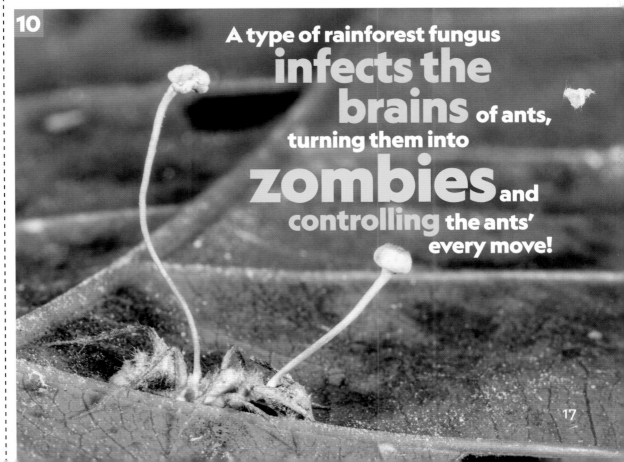

Mushrooms contain a material called chitin, which is also found in insect, crab, and lobster shells.

8

Mushrooms can be **used to make bricks and other building materials.**

9

The veins found in **blue cheese** are caused by a **type of mold.**

10

A type of rainforest fungus **infects the brains** of ants, turning them into **zombies and controlling** the ants' every move!

Shocking
Facts About
Lightning

1

There's a lake in Venezuela where lightning strikes **thousands of times a year.**

2 **Thunder** is actually the sound of **hot air vibrating** around a **lightning bolt.**

3

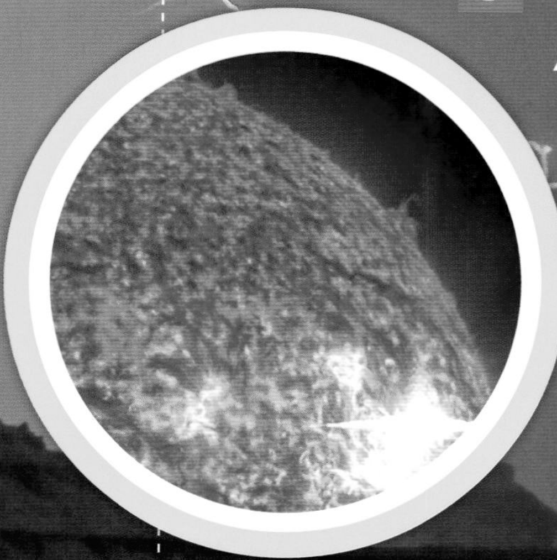

A bolt of lightning is about **five times hotter** than the surface of **the sun.**

4

Scientists think they may have discovered "dark lightning," an invisible thundercloud energy burst that's less common and way more powerful than normal lightning.

5

Dozens of lightning strikes hit the Empire State Building each year.

6

One hundred lightning bolts strike our planet each second.

7

Lightning bolts are only about as wide as a person's thumb.

8

Most lightning jumps between clouds, rather than striking the ground.

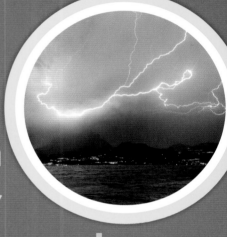

9

"Ball lightning" consists of mysterious glowing spheres that seem to float or bounce along the ground for several seconds.

10

When lightning strikes the ground, it melts minerals into a bolt-shaped fossil called a fulgurite.

Terrific Facts About Trees

1

Birch trees "sleep" at night— their branches relax and droop when it's dark and perk back up in the morning.

2

Yellow-bellied sapsuckers are small woodpeckers that drill holes in tree bark and slurp up the sap that oozes out.

3

The fruit from Osage orange trees are sometimes called "monkey brains."

5

There are hundreds of **"moon trees"** in the United States—grown from seeds that astronauts **once sent into space.**

8

Dragon's blood

trees bleed red sap when they're cut.

4

Arborists (people who take care of trees) compete for the **fastest climb** up a 60-foot (18-m) tree at the International Tree Climbing Championships.

7

People in the United States buy nearly **30 million Christmas trees each year.**

9

Thirsty trees make high-pitched **"slurping"** sounds that humans can't hear.

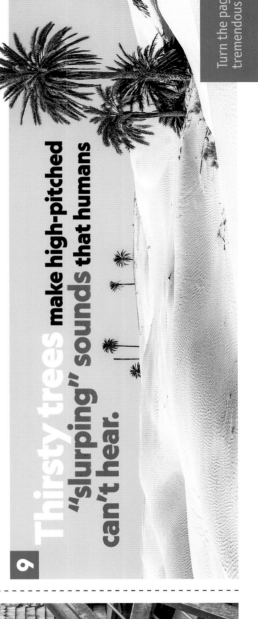

6

There's a **church inside the trunk of a tree** in France that's said to be **1,000 years old.**

A NOTRE DAME DE LA PAIX
ERIGEE PAR Mr L'ABBE
DU DETROIT, CURE
D'ALLOUVILLE en 1696

Turn the page for more tremendous tree facts!

11

The tallest tree in the world, a **redwood** nicknamed "Hyperion," is taller than the **Statue of Liberty.**

12

Orangutans spend **most of their time** in trees.

13

The poisonous manchineel tree is called *árbol de la muerte* in Spanish, meaning **"tree of death."**

10

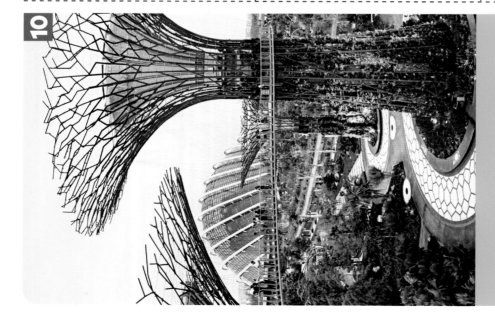

There's a grove of giant, concrete-and-steel **Supertrees** in Singapore that capture **solar energy and rainwater,** just like **real trees!**

16 One of the world's **oldest living things** is a grove of aspen trees found in Utah, U.S.A. They're estimated to be at least **80,000** years old.

18 In forests, neighboring **trees "talk"** to each other using an underground **fungus** called the **"wood wide web."**

20 Scientists who **study tree rings** are called dendrochronologists.

15 The **first species** of tree appeared between **345 and 360** million years ago.

17 Trees give off chemical signals to **warn each other** about insect attacks.

19 **One** large tree can provide **enough oxygen** for four people every day.

14 Trees **"remember"** events, even though they don't have **brains.**

1

Some fish have **taste buds** on their face.

2

The **larger the tank,** the bigger **pet goldfish can grow—** the longest goldfish ever recorded was nearly **19 inches** (47 cm) **long!**

3

When its lake dries up, an African lungfish will **dig a hole** in the mud and can **live there for months** without food or water—while breathing air.

4

Some people **catch** trout by **tickling** them!

5

You can estimate the age of some fish species by **counting the growth rings** in their scales.

6

Freshwater fish absorb water **through their skin,** but saltwater fish need to **drink water** to survive.

Fishy

Facts to Make You Move Your Fins

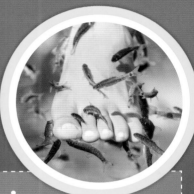

7 In some countries, you can **get a pedicure** in which **tiny fish nibble dead skin** off your feet!

8 The **biggest fish** in the world are **whale sharks,** which can grow **more than 40 feet!**
(12 m)

10 **Goldfish can learn tricks!** A fantail goldfish named Albert Einstein knew **how to play fetch,** swim through a hoop, and **play football.**

9 The **four-eyed fish** actually has two eyes, each with **two pupils:** The top pupil watches **above the water's surface** for insects and the bottom one looks **down below.**

Whale sharks

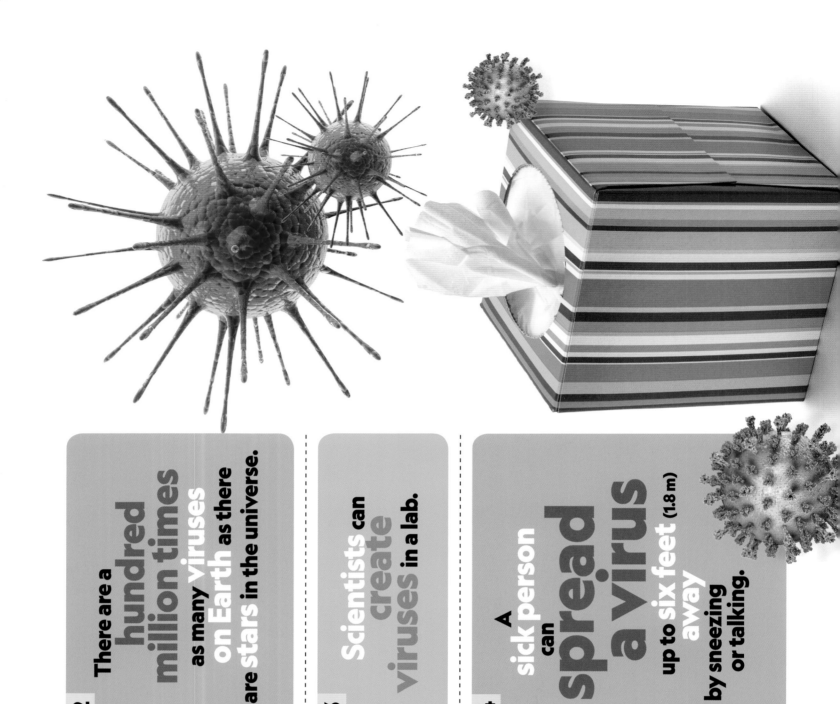

1

Each one of us has **trillions of viruses** inside our bodies at any given time, even when we're not sick.

2

There are a **hundred million times** as many viruses on Earth as there are stars in the universe.

3

Scientists can **create viruses** in a lab.

4

A sick person can **spread a virus** up to six feet (1.8 m) away by sneezing or talking.

5

Millions of common **cold viruses** could fit on the tip of a pin.

Contagious

Facts About

Viruses

8 Sunlight and specialized laser light can sometimes be used to **kill viruses.**

10 Viruses **aren't alive,** but they **aren't dead either.**

6 The word "virus" comes from the Latin word for **poisonous, slimy liquid.**

7 Eating **chicken soup** has proved to help some people get over a cold faster.

9 Scientists are hoping to use viruses **to treat acne.**

The blue dragon sea slug

uses an air bubble in its stomach to float.

1 Birds that fly long distances **lay oval eggs** or eggs with a pointy tip, while birds that fly shorter distances lay **rounder eggs.**

2 Birds **swallow** their food **whole** and then grind it up in their **gizzard,** an organ **near the stomach.**

3 There's a village in **Turkey** where people use a **language** made up of **whistles** that sound like **birdsong.**

4 The **tufts** on the heads of owls are called **plumicorns.**

5 The **biggest bird of prey** known to have existed was the Haast's eagle. Once found in **New Zealand,** this now extinct raptor had talons the size of **tiger claws.**

6 According to Norse legends, after eating a **dragon's heart,** a person could understand bird language.

Facts About Birds to Tweet About

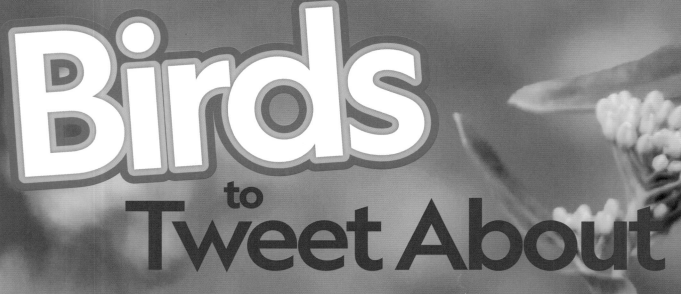

7

Some birds **practice singing** in their **dreams.**

8

Ostriches are the **only birds** that have **two toes.** Most birds have **three or four.**

9

Hundreds or thousands of **starlings** **flying in unison,** swooping and changing direction like a **cloud of smoke,** is called a **murmuration.**

10

Prehistoric birds may have **flown** using **four wings.**

Yellow wagtail

31

Sparkling
Facts About Stuff That
Shimmers and Shines

1

Scientists think our universe contains at least 100 billion galaxies, each with more than **100** billion stars.

2

The **Black Prince's Ruby,** which is set in the United Kingdom's Imperial State Crown, **isn't actually a ruby at all!** It's a gemstone called a spinel.

5

There are **opals** on **Mars.**

6

A company in France makes **lemonade** that contains **flakes** of **real gold.**

8

Salt, the **only rock** that **people eat,** was once worth as much as gold.

Turn the page for more glittering facts!

4

There's a mosque in the Middle Eastern country of Oman that contains a **crystal chandelier** that is almost the same size as a two-story house!

7

The **golden mask** of King Tutankhamun is covered with stones and glass and weighs **22 pounds** (10 kg).

3

Diamond Beach in Iceland has black sand and is dotted with chunks of **blue crystal and clear ice.**

11 There once was a Japanese hotel where guests could take a dip in a **gold bathtub**—until someone **stole it!**

10 Scientists recently disproved a belief that **magpies steal** sparkly objects and **hoard them** in their nests.

13 The **Hope Diamond,** which is blue, glows red if you shine an ultraviolet light on it.

9 Some people used to **believe that emeralds** could melt **snakes' eyes.**

12 The golden mole may be blind, but it has **fur that shimmers** in shades of blue and green.

15

Precious metals like gold and platinum may have come from **meteors** that crashed into Earth.

18

The world's **largest crystals,** found inside a cave in Mexico, weigh more than four school buses combined.

20

The mineral pyrite, which is also known as **"fool's gold,"** will give off sparks if you strike it against something hard.

14

The ancient Maya decorated their temples with paint made with **crushed mica,** a shimmery rock.

16

When disturbed, the **golden tortoise beetle's** shell turns from a metallic sheen to a yellow or red color with black spots.

17

The **world's shiniest** living thing is an African fruit that shimmers like a blue jewel.

19

The **mirror spider,** which looks like a tiny **disco ball,** has spots that reflect light, confusing predators.

Surprising
Facts About
Seeds

1

Wild bananas have seeds, unlike most farmed bananas.

2

The little **yellow dots** on the outside of a **strawberry** are actually **tiny dry fruits** that contain even **smaller seeds.**

3

The sandbox tree grows small pumpkin-shaped fruits that **explode** and **send seeds flying through the air** nearly 150 feet (46 m) from the tree.

4

The **biggest seed** in the world weighs about as much as a **bulldog!**

5

Scientists are **saving the world's seeds** in a giant **underground freezer,** called a seed vault, in Norway.

6

According to Japanese tradition, certain **cherry seeds** can **guide souls of the dead** back to their family homes.

7

A single **dandelion** plant releases more than **2,000 seeds** each year.

8

Scientists once **grew flowers** from a **32,000-year-old seed.**

9

A type of flowering grass in South Africa has **poop-scented** seeds that **fool dung beetles** into rolling them up and **planting** them in fresh soil.

10

An inventor **created Velcro** after seeing **burrs,** a type of seed, get stuck to his **dog's fur.**

Nifty Facts About Numbers

1 There's a **complex math equation** scientists use to **calculate the chances** that there's other **intelligent life** somewhere in the universe.

2 If **23 people** gather in a group, there's about a **50 percent chance** that at least **two** of them will share the **same birthday.**

3 The average dog is **about as smart** as a **two-year-old** human, can understand **165 words,** and can **count up to 4 or 5.**

4 The **first three digits** in the number pi (3.14) **spell the word "PIE"** if you read them backward in a **mirror.**

5 **Omega** is a symbol that scientists use to represent **how much "stuff"** is inside **our universe.**

6 When a **volcano erupted** on the island of Krakatoa, in present-day Indonesia, **the sound traveled** around the planet **four times.**

7 Swarms of **cicadas**—insects found across the northeastern United States—**sleep underground** and emerge only once **every 13 or 17 years.**

8 The **world's favorite number** is 7, according to one study.

9 Albert **Einstein's** birthday falls on **Pi Day**—March 14.

10 The person who **first used zero** as a **written symbol** originally wrote it as a **dot.**

Find out what gives this lake its cool colors!

The landscape in Canada's Okanagan Valley looks like a watercolor paint set, with blue, green, and yellow puddles scattered across the ground. But these water spots don't get their color from paint—instead, they're full of minerals left behind as the valley's Spotted Lake evaporates each summer.

WHAT LIES BENEATH

This lake first formed about 10,000 years ago when a glacier melted and created a depression in the ground where the lake now rests. When it rains or snows in the valley, some of the water seeps through fractures in the bedrock, which is the solid rock that sits under the surface soil, and it collects there as groundwater. This is when Spotted Lake's colorful magic happens. The valley's bedrock has a high concentration of minerals called magnesium sulfate, calcium sulfate, and sodium sulfate. As groundwater seeps through the area's bedrock, it absorbs these minerals. The mineralized water then slowly makes its way into the lake when something called hydrostatic pressure occurs. It's sort of like what happens when you try to pour more water on a very wet sponge. The sponge can't hold any more liquid, so some of it leaks out. "Think of Spotted Lake as a bubbling pot of water," geologist Murray Roed says. "The water isn't warm, but it kind of bubbles up all across the lake as the groundwater flows up into the lake."

PASS THE SALT, PLEASE

It's the introduction of these sodium-rich minerals into the lake that gives the spots their unique colors. During the spring, Spotted Lake's water is a murky brown, with the minerals just beginning to settle at the bottom. But by the summertime, most of the lake's water has evaporated. This causes the highly mineralized water that's left over to pool together into spots. The color of each pool depends on the combination of minerals and the reflection of the sun. All of the spots typically contain large amounts of each mineral, which often crystallizes, or hardens. These deposits form walkways that people could possibly stand on when the lake dries out in the late summer.

POWERFUL PUDDLES

Not that walking is recommended. The fish-free lake water is toxic if ingested. Caribou, coyotes, moose, brown bears, and bighorn sheep that live in the Okanagan Valley seem to know it and stay away from the water. Humans, however, have long recognized the healing powers of the lake. Aboriginal Canadians use the lake's mud to help soothe achy joints and other body pains. A strangely patterned body of water, an abundance of local wildlife, and mysterious healing powers? Sounds like Spotted Lake is, well, a spot worth visiting.

Caribou

The mud in Spotted Lake smells like **rotten eggs.**

Spotted Lake has about **400 spots.**

Salt patches on Mars show that the red planet may have once had **spotted lakes!**

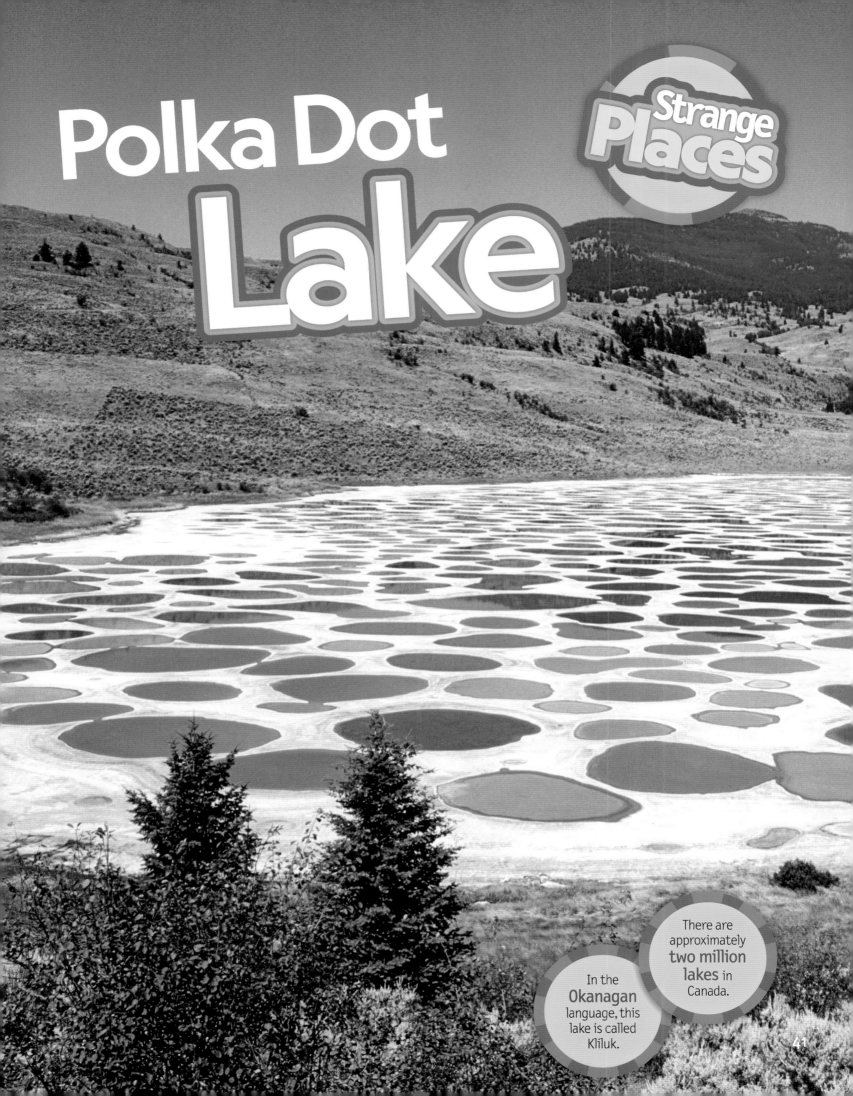

Polka Dot Lake

There are approximately **two million lakes** in Canada.

In the **Okanagan** language, this lake is called Kliluk.

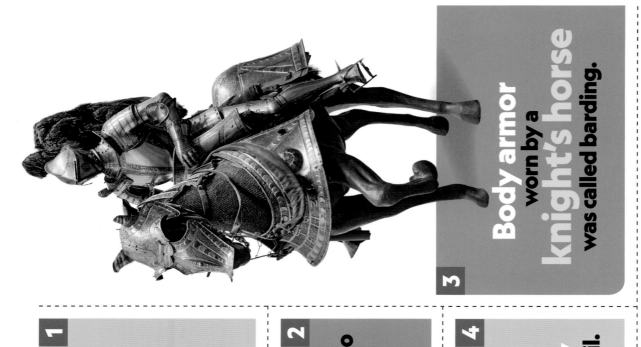

1 A medieval sword has **inscriptions** on the blade in a **language** that no one understands.

2 A **mail armor** suit was made of up to **30,000 rings** of iron, brass, or steel.

3 Body armor worn by a **knight's horse** was called barding.

4 Some knights wore **leather armor,** which was made hard and sturdy by boiling it in wax or oil.

5 A knight's armor was cleaned with **sand and urine** to keep it from rusting.

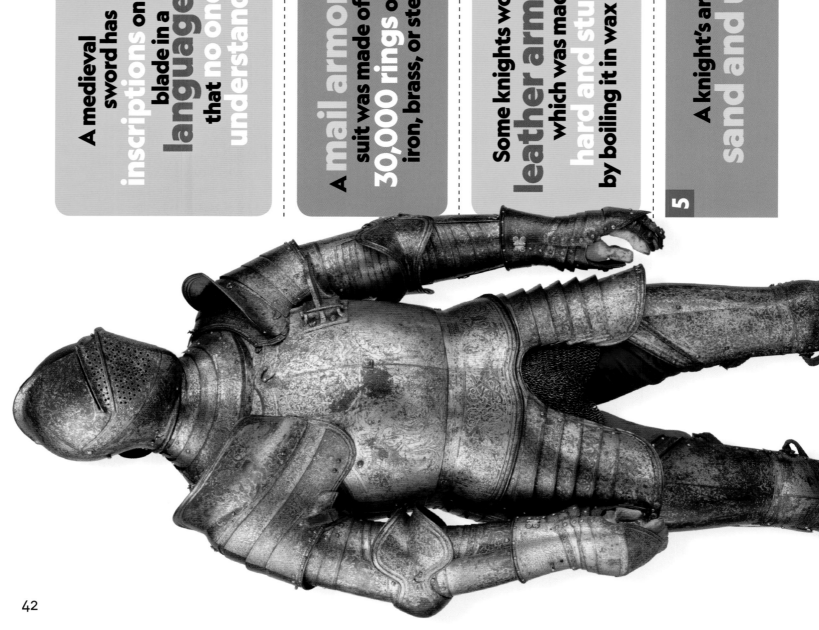

42

Amazing
Facts About

Arms & Armor

6 A suit of medieval battle armor **weighed less** than the typical equipment worn by today's firemen and infantry soldiers.

7 **Women,** including **Joan of Arc,** also likely wore armor into battle.

10 **Blue was a popular color** for medieval armor, achieved by heating the metal and then dunking it in water.

9 In the 19th century, warriors in **Kiribati,** an island nation in the Pacific, wore armor made of **coconuts and fish.**

8 A boy who began training at the age of six could become a squire by the age of 14, and a **knight** when he turned 17 or 18.

1
Sand is actually a **mixture** of **tiny shells, crystals, rocks, and corals** that have broken down over time.

2
The beach area **where waves break** is called the **swash zone.**

3
In the middle of the 1700s, **doctors** started **prescribing visits to the beach** for their **sick patients.**

4
The **white sand** found in some beaches comes from **parrotfish poop—** one large parrotfish can produce **hundreds of pounds** of sand each year!

5
In addition to **white or yellow sand** beaches, some beaches around the world have **green, purple, red, pink,** or **black** sand.

6
Over a third of the world's population lives within **a day's drive** from an **ocean.**

Soak Up These Facts About the Seashore

7 People can **dig their own hot tubs** in the sand at **Hot Water Beach** in New Zealand, where **water wells up** from an underground river that's **heated by the Earth.**

8 Some beaches are made of **"singing sand"** that **hums and squeaks.**

9 A beach can **shrink and grow** each year as winter waves **pull sand out** into the ocean and summer waves **push the sand back** onto the shore.

10 **Sand** is used to make **computer chips.**

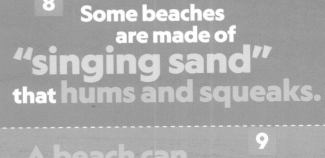

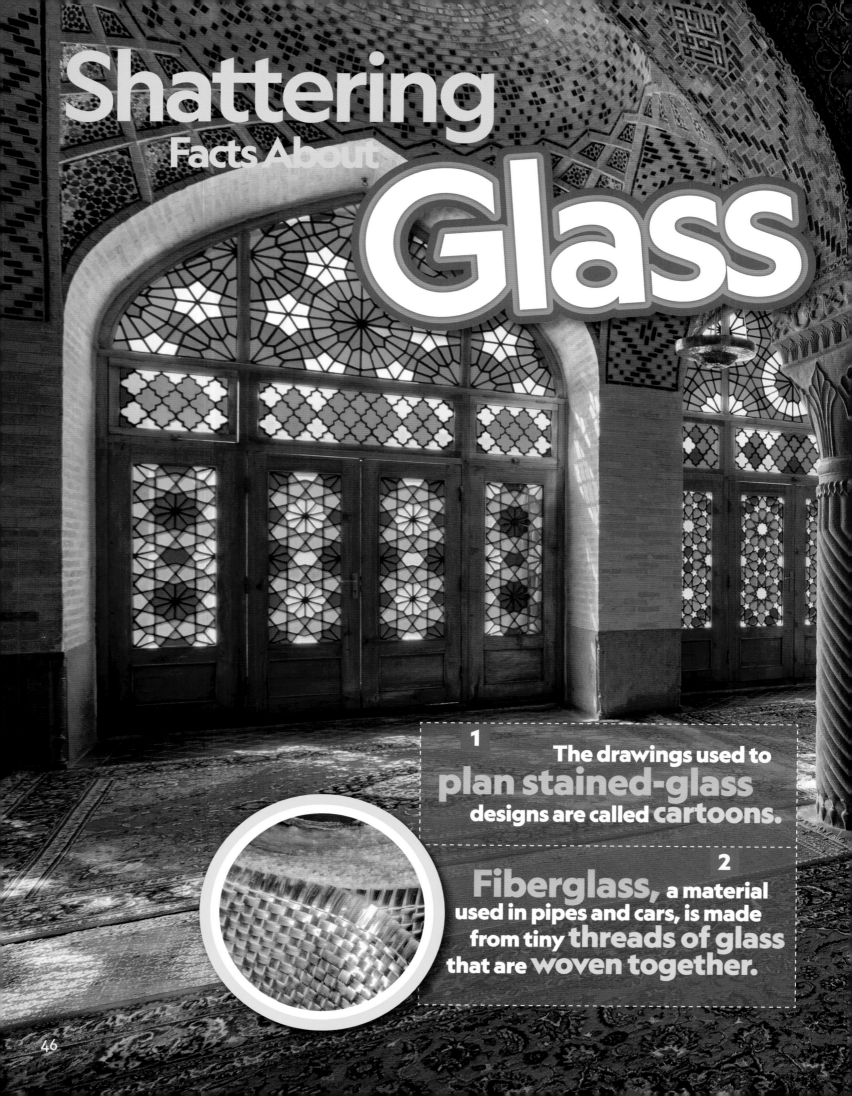

Shattering
Facts About
Glass

1
The drawings used to **plan stained-glass** designs are called **cartoons.**

2
Fiberglass, a material used in pipes and cars, is made from tiny **threads of glass** that are **woven together.**

3 Glass is **neither liquid nor solid—** it's something **in between.**

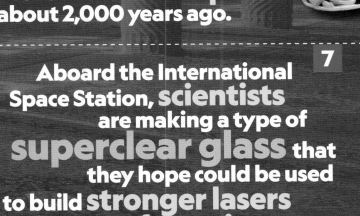

4 Toledo, Ohio, U.S.A., is nicknamed "Glass City" because workers have been **making glass there** for **more than 130 years.**

5 One of the **most valuable glass items** in the world is the Portland Vase, which was said to be made for a **Roman emperor** about 2,000 years ago.

6 Glass that erupts **from volcanoes** is called **obsidian** and is so sharp that **eye surgeons** sometimes use it instead of **steel blades.**

7 Aboard the International Space Station, **scientists** are making a type of **superclear glass** that they hope could be used to build **stronger lasers** and a **faster internet.**

8 Archaeologists have found **pieces of glass** made by **humans** about **3,250 years ago.**

9 Glass can form when **lightning strikes** sand.

10 The first **contact lenses** were **made from glass.**

47

1 There is a **massive storm** on Jupiter that **has lasted** for the past **150 years** and could fit **three Earths** inside it.

2 The TRAPPIST-1 dwarf star, which **has seven Earth-size planets** orbiting it, could be up to **twice as old** as our solar system!

3 Scientists named 60 discoveries of baby moons and clumps of ice and rock after **kitten names:** Fluffy, Socks, and Whiskers, to name a few!

4 **Saturn's moon** Mimas is sometimes referred to as the **Death Star** because its shape resembles the popular *Star Wars* spacecraft.

5 On August 21, 1924, there was a national day of **radio silence** so scientists could use a **radio receiver** to listen for **alien signals from Mars.**

6 Some astronauts say **space smells** like **burned steak.**

7 GJ 504b is a **large pink planet** that orbits within a system that scientists estimate is about **160 million years old.**

8 The Boomerang Nebula is the **coldest known object** in the universe at **nearly minus 460°F** (-270°C).

9

A quasar is an object that is **similar to a star,** but it is **so bright** that it **drowns out the light** from the other stars in its galaxy.

10

In 2019, **NASA's New Horizons spacecraft** visited an **icy object** located about **4 billion miles** (6.5 billion km) **from Earth** that may have formed more than **4.5 billion years ago.**

Rocket-Fueled
Facts About
Space

1 Cinnabar is one of the **most toxic** minerals on Earth— it's often referred to as **"dragon's blood."**

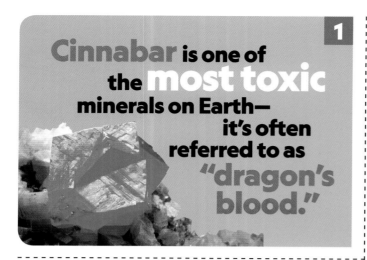

2 The **sandstone** in **Vermilion Cliffs National Monument** in Arizona, U.S.A., **appears to change color** throughout the day.

3 The **first lasers** were made from artificial **ruby crystals.**

5 **"Garnet"** comes from a **Latin word** that translates to **"pomegranate."**

4 Scientists believe that in billions of years, **the sun will become** one **huge diamond.**

Facts That **Totally** Rock

6 **Tourmaline** is also known as the **"rainbow gem"** because it comes in **every color!**

7 A group of over 1,500 **limestone mounds** in the Philippines are called the **Chocolate Hills.**

8 More than **50,000 people** a year head to **Emerald Hollow Mine** in North Carolina, U.S.A., to **dig for emeralds.** Finders keepers!

9 The **skinny rock formations** left over from **volcanic eruptions** in Göreme National Park in Turkey are known as **"fairy chimneys."**

10 **Endoliths** are tiny living organisms that **live inside rocks,** giving a whole new meaning to the idea of a **pet rock.**

Ultrahot
Facts About
Fire

1

Sometimes wildfires **form their own tornadoes,** called **firenados.**

2

Fire isn't an object— it's an event caused by a chemical reaction in a mixture of gases.

3 Fires with **more oxygen** are blue and burn the **hottest**; fires with **less oxygen** are yellow and **burn the coolest.**

4 Wildfires can create **their own storm clouds,** called flammagenitus or pyrocumulus clouds.

5 The chemicals in **pistachios give off heat,** so if too many of the nuts are packaged together they can actually **burst into flames.**

6 The remains of the **oldest known campfire** are about **one million years old.**

7 Earth is the **only known planet** in our solar system **where fire occurs.**

8 The **Olympic torch** is lit with a **curved mirror** that focuses the sun's rays into a **superhot beam.**

9 A **coal fire** under a mountain in Australia has been **burning continuously** for **6,000 years.**

10 Fireworks get their colors from chemicals: Strontium and lithium **burn red,** calcium **burns orange,** sodium **burns yellow,** barium **burns green,** and copper **burns blue.**

FLOATING UMBRELLAS

WHAT Umbrella art

WHERE Águeda, Portugal

DETAILS Paging Mary Poppins! As part of an art festival called AgitÁgueda, hundreds of parasols were seen floating above this Portuguese street. Though they looked like they were suspended in midair, the umbrellas were actually held in place by wires connected to buildings on both sides of the street. Nothing's going to rain on this artistic parade.

Extreme Weirdness

SEA CREATURES ROCK OUT

WHAT Underwater band

WHERE Beijing, China

DETAILS Talk about making a splash! Musicians wearing marine animal costumes grooved inside a giant, water-filled tank at the Beijing Aquarium to celebrate the Chinese New Year. Billed as the country's first underwater band, they entertained the visitors—and maybe the fish, too.

ICE CUBE ON WHEELS

WHAT Truck made of ice

WHERE Hensall, Canada

DETAILS It's going to be an icy ride. This functional truck has a body made of more than 11,000 pounds (nearly 5,000 kg) of ice. Built over a base frame with wheels, the icy exterior covers a real engine, brakes, and steering wheel. It runs on a battery that's specially designed to start in frigid conditions that would keep most cars from revving up. The car can only go short distances—but what a great place to chill!

RUNNING OF THE APES

WHAT Great Gorilla Run

WHERE London, England

DETAILS On your mark, get set, go-rilla! Over a thousand runners put on furry costumes to run across London's Tower Bridge as part of the Great Gorilla Run. The annual event raises money to help save the primate species from extinction. Now that's a cause to go ape for.

UNDERWATER DINING

WHAT Aquarium-dining divers

WHERE London, England

DETAILS There's seafood and then there's undersea-food. Divers at a London aquarium enjoyed an underwater fish supper with a green sea turtle to promote sustainable fishing practices. Their goal was to encourage the protection of overfished marine life such as Atlantic salmon. Looks like the event went swimmingly.

KERMIT SALUTES STATUE

WHAT Mexico City's summer celebration

WHERE Mexico City, Mexico

DETAILS It's easy being green when you're the star of the parade. A giant Kermit the Frog balloon floated by the capital's famous Angel of Independence monument as part of a parade to welcome summer. The Muppet was joined by the likes of Mickey Mouse and Spider-Man. Who knew frogs could fly?

Smooth
Facts About
Silk

2

Spider silk is so strong that it's often compared to steel.

3

The **thread** in a silkworm **cocoon** can be up to **a mile long.**
(1.6 km)

1

According to Chinese legends, silk was first discovered when a **silkworm cocoon** fell into the **empress's cup of tea** and **unraveled** to reveal a **single thread.**

4

Some types of **crickets** can **make silk.**

5

Some **Vikings** used silk to decorate their **burial ships.**

6

Golden orb weaving spiders spin **yellow silk.**

7

Researchers have **discovered prehistoric silk** in 8,500-year-old **tombs.**

8

Silkworms are actually **caterpillars,** not worms.

9

The first hot air balloon that carried people **took off** in 1783 and was made of **paper and silk.**

10

During World War II, to help imprisoned soldiers escape, **British spies sent maps** printed on **foldable silk** inside ordinary-looking objects.

Sugar-Coated

Facts About Candy

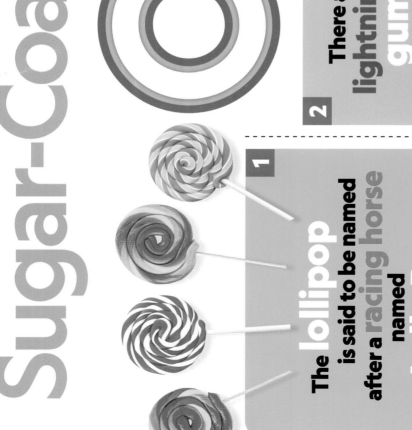

1 The lollipop is said to be named after a racing horse named Lolly Pop.

2 There are lightning bug gummy candies that actually light up when squeezed.

3 In 1969, the astronauts of the Apollo 9 space mission nicknamed one module of their spacecraft Gumdrop.

4 Gum chewing may improve test scores.

Turn the page for more sweet candy facts!

7

You can buy **wasabi-flavored Kit Kat bars** in Japan.

9

There's a **marshmallow festival** in Indiana, U.S.A., every year, with games, a marshmallow bake-off, and a pizza-eating contest with **marshmallow toppings!**

6

Salsagheti is a sweet and spicy spaghetti-like gummy candy that comes with a sauce to pour over the **"noodles."**

8

The first **bubblegum,** made in 1906, was called **Blibber-Blubber.**

5

The largest **bubble-gum bubble** ever recorded to date was **20 inches** (51 cm) in diameter—that's twice the diameter of a basketball!

11

Candy didn't become a part of celebrating **Halloween** until the 1950s.

12

The word **"sweetmeats,"** used in the United Kingdom, refers to treats made of sugar or covered in sugar.

15

Germans eat more candy on average than citizens from any other country.

10

Salt Lake City, Utah, U.S.A., **eats the most Jell-O** of any city in the entire world.

13

At U.S. president Ronald Reagan's inauguration, attendees ate more than three tons (2.7 t) of red, white, and blue **jelly beans.**

14

The man who **invented cotton candy** was a dentist.

16

Tootsie Rolls were added to soldiers' rations during World War II because they didn't melt.

17

A 5,000-year-old piece of chewing gum was discovered in Finland!

18

Enough **candy corn** is made every year to give **every person on Earth** one kernel.

19

According to a survey, most people eat the ears off of their chocolate **Easter bunnies** before they eat anything else.

20

Fashion stylists once made a dress out of **50,000 gummy bears**—it weighed 220 pounds! (100 kg)

1 The **Southern Cross** constellation appears on **Brazilian coins.**

2 Scientists found a **32,000-year-old** carving on an **ivory tablet** of an object that could represent the **Orion constellation.**

3 **Most of the names** for today's **constellations** came from the **ancient Greeks.**

4 The **Big Dipper** is not actually a **constellation** but an **asterism,** a group of stars that are part of a **larger constellation.**

5 The **North Star** is the brightest star in the constellation **Ursa Minor,** also known as the **Little Bear.**

6 There are **88 constellations** visible in **Earth's sky.**

7 The **largest constellation** is **Hydra,** which is in the **shape of a water snake.**

8 Some experts believe that the **ancient Egyptians** used the position of the **constellations** to decide **where to build** their temples and monuments.

9 The **Chinese zodiac** calendar may be based on the **path of Jupiter** as it crosses different **constellations** during the year.

10 The **brightest star** in the constellation **Leo** is actually made up of **four separate stars.**

Cosmic
Facts About
Constellations

Pizza
Facts By the Slice

1

A
rooftop pizzeria
in Cuba delivers its pies by
lowering them in baskets
to customers
waiting on the sidewalk
below.

2

Italy
passed a law requiring
that any Margherita pizza
must use **specific types**
of flour, yeast, and cheese,
and the dough must be
kneaded by hand.

3

Ancient Greeks made the
first food
to resemble pizza—a circle
of bread with toppings,
but no tomato sauce.

4

In the United States,
National Pizza Day
is on February 9.

In Scotland, pizza is sometimes dipped in batter and **deep-fried.**

5

Las Vegas, Nevada, U.S.A., hosts an annual **Pizza Convention** where competitors juggle spinning pizza dough discs **while dancing to music.**

6

Because of the **tomato sauce,** a slice of pizza counts as a **serving of vegetables** in school lunches **in the United States.**

8

7

The **most expensive pizza** is made **with black squid ink dough, truffle oil, caviar, Stilton cheese,** and **edible gold flakes.**

9

The **biggest pizza** ever made was **2.5 times as big as a basketball court.**

10

Pac-Man's shape was inspired by a whole pizza with a slice removed.

Cool Facts
About
Copycats

1 **Cuttlefish** sometimes **imitate hermit crabs** to **sneak up** on fish and to look **less appetizing** to predators.

2 Opossums **play dead** and give off a special **rotting scent** to **trick predators** into walking away.

3 **Bee orchids** have **petals** that **look like bees** to attract **pollinators**.

4 To **scare off enemies,** burrowing owl chicks give off a **rattling hiss** similar to that of **rattlesnakes.**

5 Blue jays **can scream** like **hawks.**

6 An **insect** called the female orchid mantis **pretends to be a flower** to catch prey.

7 California **ground squirrels** chew up rattlesnake skins and **cover themselves in the goo** to hide their **natural scent.**

8 In the Amazon jungle, **margay cats lure prey** by copying the call of **monkeys** they like to eat.

9 **Dogs** can **mimic** some **human gestures.**

10 The lithops plant **blends in** with its environment by **looking like a rock.**

What's the Difference?

Check out these similar pairings and see how you can determine this from that!

CRAYFISH VS. LOBSTER

Crayfish might look like small lobsters, but there's more to each of these creatures than meets the eye. These pinchy critters are both arthropods, which means that they wear their skeletons on the outside of their bodies, as do crabs, shrimp, and their land-dwelling counterparts, insects and arachnids. Lobsters and crayfish look similar, too: They both have five pairs of legs, five pairs of tiny limbs called swimmerets, and one pair of larger claws, including one claw for cutting and the other for crushing. However, lobsters are big and live in salt water, while crayfish are small and live in freshwater lakes, streams, rivers, and ponds. Crayfish also build water-filled underground tunnels during the fall and winter seasons, whereas lobsters spend their time on the ocean floor. Whether you find yourself face to face with a crayfish or a lobster, keep your hands away from their claws!

VITAMIN VS. MINERAL

We get both of these in our food, and we find them in gummy vitamin supplements. But what is the difference between a vitamin and a mineral? And why do we need them at all? The answer is that, apart from vitamin D, these supplements contain molecules your body cannot make on its own. Vitamins are made by plants and other animals. Some of these dissolve in fat, which means your body can store them, but others dissolve in water, which means that anything you don't use gets washed out when you pee, so you need to replace these vitamins every day. Minerals, however, are elements that come from rocks and soil and get absorbed by plants, which then pass minerals up the food chain. Some animals, like goats, get minerals by chewing rocks and licking salt. Thankfully, humans only need to spend some time in the sun, eat healthy foods, and take the occasional gummy supplement to get these nutrients!

TOAD VS. FROG

They may look a lot alike and have one happy hop, but frogs and toads are different characters. If you're in doubt about what to call one of these amphibians, stick with "frog," since that broad category includes all toads. Otherwise, the rule of thumb for distinguishing between the two is this: Frogs hop on long legs and have smooth, wet-looking skin. Toads are a subcategory of frogs that crawl on short legs and have dry, bumpy skin. Frogs are more likely to be seen in moist habitats. Toads are more likely to be seen in dry habitats. With so many differences, can frogs and toads in nature really be friends? Unfortunately, in nature you are more likely to see them hunting each other than to see them sharing a friendly swim!

SEAL VS. SEA LION VS. SEA OTTER

There are a few things that set these three adorable, brown, furry swimmers apart. Seals and sea lions belong to a group called pinnipeds, meaning "fin foot." Pinnipeds have a thick layer of blubber under their furry skin to stay warm. One of the most obvious differences between them is the size and position of their flippers. Sea lions are covered in skin and have long flippers that they use to lift themselves off the ground to "walk." Seals, on the other hand, are covered in fur and have short flippers that can't lift the seal's body, so seals move on the ground like caterpillars. Sea lions also have visible earflaps, but seals do not. When it comes to sea otters, they belong to the same group as weasels, have paws rather than flippers, and stay warm under a thick fur coat.

NOCTURNAL VS. CREPUSCULAR

There are lots of reasons to sleep during the day if you're a nocturnal animal. It's usually cooler at night, which is important if you live in a place that gets very hot or very dry. Small nocturnal mammals also forage or hunt for food because the cover of darkness makes it harder for predators to see them. Badgers, bats, fennec foxes, and sloths that are active at night are nocturnal, and their eyes are especially good at seeing in dim light. But midnight shenanigans aren't a good fit for everyone. Creatures like cats, deer, opossums, and fireflies can do well by hunting and socializing during crepuscule, which is just before sunrise or sunset. At this time of day, fewer predators may be about, and the foods they prefer are easier to snatch.

Sea lions

Radiant
Facts About
Rainbows

1 Scientists used a laser to create a **repeating rainbow**—resulting in 200 rainbows **stacked on top** of one another.

2 There's a **mountain in Peru** that has **rainbow-colored stripes.**

4 Scientists think there might be rainbows **on Saturn's moon Titan.**

3 The order of colors in a rainbow is **always red on top** and violet on the bottom, unless it's a double rainbow, in which case the colors of the second rainbow **are flipped.**

Triple and quadruple rainbows exist in nature.

5

6 A rainbow actually has **100 million colors,** but most people can only **see one million** different colors.

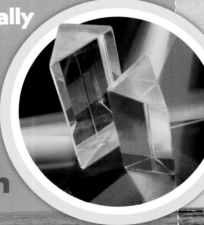

7 It's almost **impossible** to see a **full rainbow** in the sky at noon.

8 Rainbows **have no end—** they are **circles.**

9 If you **look out** the window of an **airplane,** sometimes you can see **rainbow rings,** called "glories," on the surface of **clouds.**

10 Rainbows are **even wider** than what we can see. There are certain wavelengths **we can't see** as color that extend **beyond** the red and violet bands.

Dazzling
Facts About
Deserts

1
Desert-dwelling
fennec
foxes
never have to
drink water.

2
Tumbleweeds,
a common desert
plant, are originally
from Russia.

3

Deserts **aren't always hot—** temperatures in Mongolia's Gobi can drop to **nearly -29°F** (-34°C)— almost as cold as winter temperatures on **Mount Everest.**

4

Deserts that get unusually **heavy rainfall** sometimes experience a **"super bloom"** of flowers that open **almost overnight.**

5

Satellite pictures show that there **used to be** an **enormous river** flowing through the **Sahara desert.**

6

Any place that gets **less than** **10 inches** (25 cm) **of rain each year** is considered a desert.

7

Some parts of Chile's Atacama Desert have **never had recorded rainfall.**

8

The Gobi is **growing bigger** each year. In China, they've planted a **"Great Green Wall"—** more than **66 billion trees—** to hold the desert back.

9

Deserts cover more than **one-fifth** of our **planet's surface.**

10

A large field of **sand dunes** is **called an erg.**

Facts About Lava to Warm Up To

1

When lava flows fast, it hardens into rough, **craggy chunks** called aa. When lava flows slowly, it forms **smooth rolls** and shiny coils called **pahoehoe.**

2

Lava **temperatures** can range from **1300 to 2300°F** (700 to 1250°C).

3

It's considered **bad luck** to **remove lava rocks** from the Hawaiian Islands.

4

Below Earth's crust, there are **giant blobs** of mysterious **molten metal** that rise and sink like a super slow **lava lamp.**

5

Half-pipes have been **carved by lava flows** at a ski resort near an **active volcano** in Chile.

6

People use **pumice stones** to **scrub off dead skin** from their bodies, but these special stones are actually **pieces of lava** that erupted underwater and **floated to the surface.**

7

There's a volcano in Tanzania, Africa, that spews a **rare type of lava** that **turns silver when it cools.**

8

Sometimes when small drops of liquid lava are **blown by the wind,** they transform into **golden threads** known as **Pele's hair.**

9

Half of CoRoT-7b—a planet **489 light-years** away from Earth— is covered with an **ocean of lava.**

10

Lava is the term for **magma** (molten rock) that **reaches the surface of the planet.**

Scaly Facts
About
Reptiles

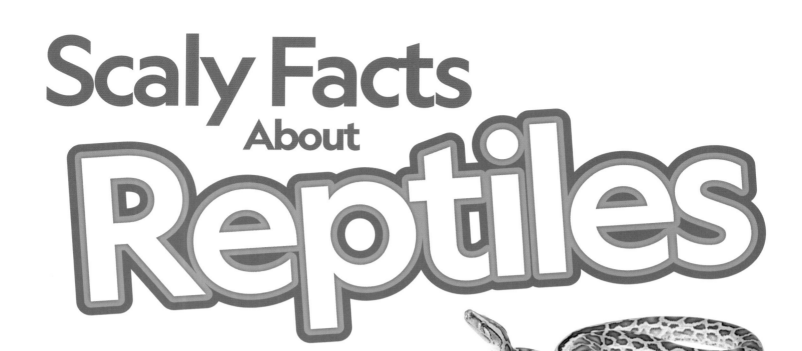

1 **Pink iguanas** live on an island in the Galápagos.

2 In the Florida Everglades, U.S.A., pet **Burmese pythons** released into the wild **can grow so big** that they constrict and **eat alligators.**

3 Some snakes are able to **glide through the air** between tree branches, almost as if they're **flying!**

4 A **crocodile** grows up to **3,000 teeth** in its lifetime.

5 Basilisk lizards **can run** on the **surface of water.**

6 **Anole** lizards **do push-ups** as a warning to other lizards.

7 A **chameleon's tongue** **can shoot** out of its mouth and **grab an insect** faster than you can blink your eyes.

8 **Ancient** snakes **had legs!** Today's pythons and boa constrictors have **tiny leg bones** in the muscles **near their tails.**

9 A **turtle's shell** is covered in **bony plates** called scutes, which are made of the same material as **human fingernails.**

10 Scientists are studying **Komodo dragon blood** to possibly **make medicine** for humans.

1 The United States military **fed soldiers** peanut butter and jelly sandwiches **during World War II.**

2 College students in Philadelphia, Pennsylvania, U.S.A., set a **world record** by making **49,100** peanut butter and jelly sandwiches **in one hour.**

3 In space, **astronauts** make peanut butter and jelly sandwiches with **tortillas**, using **tape** and **Velcro** to hold supplies down.

4 **April 2** is **National Peanut Butter and Jelly** Day in the United States.

5 The **world's largest** PB&J sandwich **weighed** nearly as much as a **large male polar bear.**

6 The average **American eats 1,500** PB&J sandwiches **before they graduate** high school.

7

Peanut butter used to be served on sandwiches with **pimento cheese,** celery, cucumbers, and **edible flowers.**

8

The **first recorded recipe** for PB&J was published in a cookbook **in 1901.**

9

In the early 1900s, peanut butter sandwiches were served to **wealthy people.**

10

A favorite **pregame snack** of many pro basketball players is a PB&J sandwich.

Finger-Licking Facts About **Peanut Butter and Jelly**

1

Butterflies **hide** under leaves or mushrooms **when it rains.**

2

If the outside temperature is **below 60°F** (16°C), butterflies must **warm their wings** in the sun **before flying.**

3

A **group** of butterflies is sometimes **called a flutter.**

4

Blue morpho butterflies aren't actually blue. Their wings have **tiny prisms** that reflect light, making them **appear blue.**

5

Butterflies live on **every continent** of the world **except Antarctica.**

6

Butterflies **taste** with **their feet.**

7

Butterflies **can remember** things they **learned as caterpillars,** even though their **brains turn to goo** during metamorphosis.

8

Some caterpillars **can disguise** themselves as ants.

9

Butterflies suck up the **nutrients they need** from **moist dirt, dead animals,** and **even poop,** a behavior **called mud puddling.**

10

Some butterflies have ears on their wings.

Fluttering
Facts About
Butterflies

Checkered swallowtail

Dreamy

Facts to Sleep On

1

Some people **dream in black and white.**

2

Some scientists **believe that babies start to dream before they're born.**

3

The invention of the sewing machine, Google, and Einstein's theory of relativity were all ideas inspired by dreams.

4

Our brains can solve complex problems— like how to fix something, or how to handle a disagreement with someone— **while we're dreaming.**

Dreaming can improve your memory. 5

6 According to one study, **eating cheese** before bed can cause people to have **weird** dreams.

Most people **dream** at least **four to six** times a night.
8

People who **wake up** during a **dream** are more likely to **remember it.**
9

7 Some people are **able to control** what happens in **their dreams.** This type of dreaming is called lucid dreaming or **"dream yoga."**

10 Surveys show that some of the **most common dreams** are about **falling, being chased,** teachers or school situations, and **flying.**

Frigid Facts About the Arctic

1

Every year around **December 21,** the night in the Arctic Circle is so long there's **no sunrise,** and around **June 21,** the day is so long there's **no sunset.**

2

Some dinosaurs lived in the Arctic.

3

One extra-furry species of **bumblebee** survives in the Arctic by **shivering** to stay warm.

4

Eight nations have territory in the **Arctic Circle:** Canada, Russia, the United States, Iceland, Greenland, Norway, Finland, and Sweden.

5

Clouds created by **rising gas from bird poop** may help to keep the Arctic cool.

Polar bear

6

The **average winter temperature** in the Arctic is about **minus 40°F** (-40°C).

7

The name **"Arctic"** comes from the **Greek word** for **bear,** *arktos.*

8

The **Arctic Ocean** is the **shallowest ocean** on Earth.

9

Arctic terns fly more than **a million miles** (1.6 million km) in their lifetimes—that's the same distance as making **three round-trip** flights to **the moon.**

10

If you hold **a compass** while standing directly over the **magnetic North Pole,** the arrow will **stop working, spin randomly,** or point to something magnetic on **your body.**

Walt Disney modeled Sleeping Beauty's castle after Neuschwanstein Castle in Germany.

6 During the 1800s, Great Britain's **Queen Victoria** was **a huge fan of photography.** She learned to develop her own pictures and had a private darkroom built in Buckingham Palace.

2 The **first popular camera** sold to everyday consumers was called the Kodak Brownie, and it cost only $1!

3 The **first photograph**—taken in 1826—was black and white and took several hours to develop.

5 The **first photograph was called a "sun drawing."**

1 Photos of a **galloping horse,** showing that its **feet are off the ground mid-stride,** were an inspiration for the invention of movies in the late 1800s.

4 Astronauts left **12 cameras** behind on the surface of the moon to save weight on the trip back to Earth.

Picture

These Facts About Photography

7 A chemist named Robert Cornelius took his own picture—the first selfie—in 1839.

8 Patrick Peterson, a professional football player, holds the world record for most selfies taken in an hour: 1,449!

9 World Photo Day is August 19.

10 Over one billion photos are shared on social media every day.

1 Mucus, snot, mucilage, ectoplasm, and **gloop** are all names for **slime.**

2 Velvet worms **shoot slime** out of the sides of their heads to **trap their prey.**

3 Maggot slime can be used to help **heal wounds.**

4 Snail slime is added to some products used to **soften skin.**

5 If a predator attacks, a **hagfish** will release **gallons of slime** to attempt to **choke the attacker.**

6 Parrotfish **sleep in a bubble** of **mucus** at night.

7 The **yellow slime mold** *Fuligo septica* is often called **"scrambled egg"** or **"dog vomit"** slime mold.

8 Government researchers once developed a **"sticky foam gun"** that would **stop criminals** by **shooting slime.**

9 The **human body** can **make enough mucus** every day to fill an **ostrich egg.**

10 Sea creatures called larvaceans **build a slimy "house"** around themselves **to catch** microscopic **bits of food** in the water.

Squishy Facts About Slime

Outrageous Facts About Everything Under Our Feet

1 **Soil** is more than just dirt—it includes so many microbes and bugs that some scientists actually say **it's alive.**

2 Scientists estimate that more than **a quarter of all living species** can be found in soils.

3 You **won't sink** underground if you step in **quicksand**—humans will only sink up to **their waist.**

4

Disney World is built over a **network of tunnels,** commonly called a **utilidor.**

5

There's one **ant colony** that has built vast **underground cities** on **every continent** except Antarctica.

6

There could be a **massive body of water** that lies deep below Earth's surface— a body **three times** larger than all Earth's **oceans** put together.

7

Rivers that used to be aboveground now flow **underneath New York City.**

8

You can ride an **underground Ferris wheel** in Romania.

9

Police found an **abandoned movie theater** in the **catacombs** underneath Paris, where miles of tunnels are lined with **skulls and bones.**

10

Elephants send low-frequency **vibration messages** to each other **through the ground.**

Razor-Sharp Towers Hide a Wild World

A forbidding forest of pointed peaks soars above the surrounding jungle landscape. This surreal limestone lair looks like a challenge straight out of a video game. The eye-popping spot—called Tsingy de Bemaraha national park and reserve—is located in western Madagascar, an island off the southeast coast of Africa.

It's easy to see why the word "tsingy" (pronounced sing-EE) means "where one cannot walk barefoot" in the local Malagasy language. But in this brutal landscape, many creatures make their home among these stone towers where only a few humans dare to set foot.

Von der Decken's sifakas

One **species of gecko** in Madagascar looks like a **dead leaf.**

The **aye-aye lemur** was once thought to be **extinct.**

90% of the species found in Madagascar are found **nowhere else** on Earth.

WATER AT WORK

Around 200 million years ago, the limestone plateau that makes up Tsingy de Bemaraha was part of the seabed. Over millions of years, the limestone layers below the water slowly rose above the sea level. Heavy rains continually sculpted the land, altering its shape. "When rainwater flows into cracks in the landscape, it dissolves the rock," says Márton Veress, a geomorphologist (someone who studies the evolution of the Earth's surface). The constant dissolution created crevasses, or deep open cracks, across the top layer of land. Over time, the tops of the rocks sharpened into the knife-like points visible today.

CREATURE FEATURES

You won't find many humans venturing among those spiky limestone towers—just a few locals, plus some brave scientists and tourists with rugged rock-climbing gear. But you'll spot plenty of animals in the park. "The biodiversity of Tsingy de Bemaraha is unique even when compared to the rest of Madagascar, which hosts many animals found nowhere else on the planet," primatologist Travis Steffens says. "The tsingy is like its own separate island within an island." That's because the wildlife of Tsingy de Bemaraha had to adapt to the park's challenging surroundings, learning to survive everywhere from large dry forests to dense jungle-like tropical areas that sprouted up through crevasses in the landscape. Lemurs in particular thrive in the tsingy—11 species call it home. Six of those species are endangered. Among them is the white-furred Von der Decken's sifaka, which developed powerful hind legs to leap up to 30 feet (9 m) from peak to peak. Its hands have developed soft pads that allow it to grip the rocks as it clings vertically and leaps across the park's spikes. Even the plants have adapted to life in the unusual tsingy. For example, xerophytes (pronounced ZEE-roh-fites) found in the tsingy's dry forests can stretch their long, rope-like roots into various parts of the rock face in search of water.

MORE TO EXPLORE

There's still so much to uncover in this strange and stunning no-man's-land, and scientists continue to encounter new plant and animal species as they study the park. Who knows what new discoveries await those brave enough to venture into Tsingy de Bemaraha's treacherous terrain?

Stone Forest

Dancing lemurs can't walk on all fours—they hop sideways.

Madagascar is home to baobab trees more than 1,000 years old.

Facts About Fur, Feathers, Skin, and Scales

2 Flamingos are born with gray or white feathers that turn pink over time because of the algae and shrimp the birds eat.

1 You shed your entire outer layer of skin about once a month.

3 Some geckos and lizards eat their skin after they shed it.

Turn the page for more cool facts on coverings!

5

A square inch (6.5 sq cm) of human skin contains about 1,000 **nerve endings.**

6

Chameleons can change their color because of special light-reflecting crystals in their skin.

8

The **ancient Maya** used the bright green and blue feathers of the **quetzal** bird as **currency.**

4

Special **jagged feathers on owls' wings** help muffle noise, allowing them to fly almost silently.

7

Dogs are born with **fuzzy fur** known as a **puppy coat,** which is replaced by a thicker adult coat within a few months.

9

Some people are born with **blue skin.**

11 Fish scales are an ingredient used in some lipsticks.

12 Hippos are protected from sunburn by a sticky orange and red oil they secrete from sweat glands all over their skin.

10 Baby dolphins are born with whiskers on their chins.

13 Any animal that has bare skin—humans, whales, even cats and dogs (on their noses)—can get sunburned.

14 Some people are born without fingerprints.

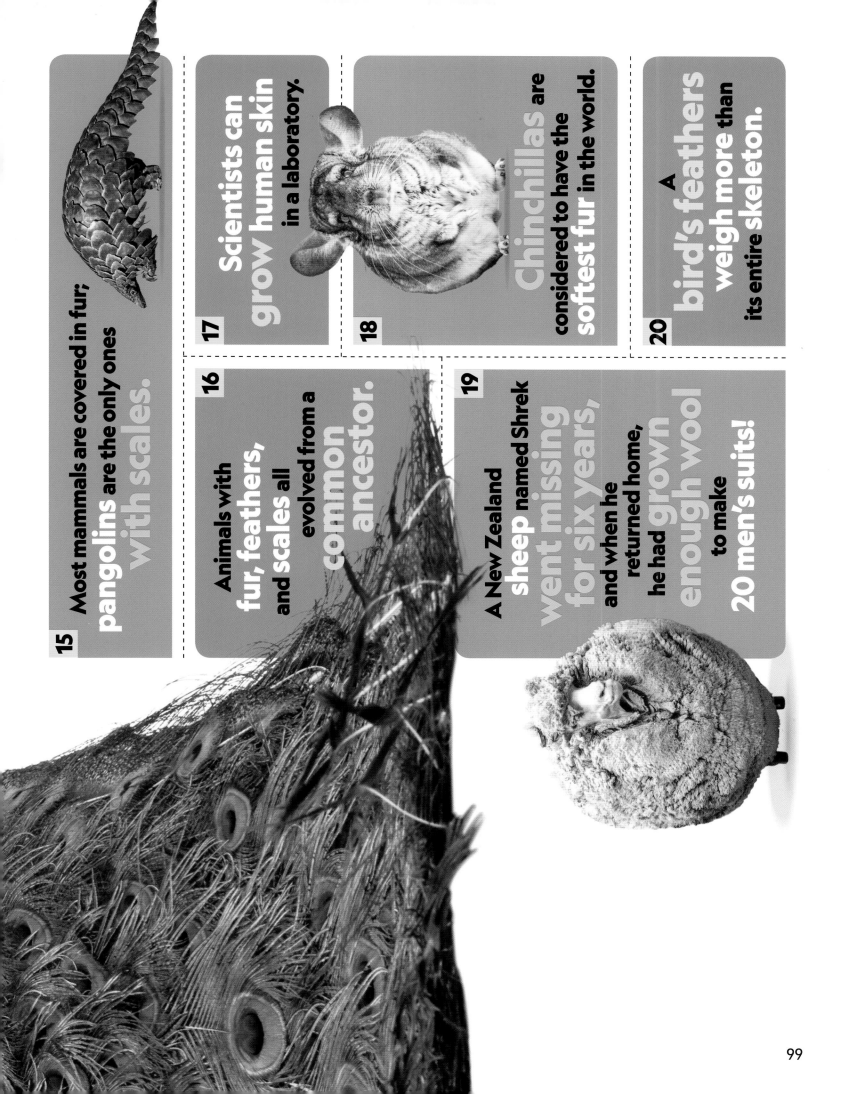

15 Most mammals are covered in fur; pangolins are the only ones **with scales.**

16 Animals with **fur, feathers, and scales all** evolved from a **common ancestor.**

17 Scientists can **grow human skin** in a laboratory.

18 Chinchillas are considered to have the **softest fur** in the world.

19 A New Zealand **sheep** named Shrek **went missing for six years,** and when he returned home, he had **grown enough wool** to make **20 men's suits!**

20 A **bird's feathers** **weigh more than** its entire skeleton.

Wild Facts

About Places That Thrill

1

The Formula Rossa in Abu Dhabi, United Arab Emirates, is the **world's fastest roller coaster,** speeding to **149 miles an hour** (240 km/h) **in under five seconds.**

2

Tropical Islands Resort, Germany, is the **world's largest indoor water park,** with speedy waterslides plus the world's largest **indoor rainforest.**

3

At a theme park in Nantes, France, you **can ride** on a 40-foot (12-m)-tall **mechanical elephant** that walks through the park.

4 The original map that Walt Disney created for **Disneyland** sold for $708,000.

5 At Crocosaurus Cove in Australia, **you can swim** in a clear tube next to a **16-foot** (4.9-m)-**long saltwater crocodile.**

6 One water park in the Bahamas has a 60-foot (18-m) **waterslide** that shoots riders through a **see-through** tunnel with dozens of **real sharks** swimming around it!

7 Aqualud park in France is home to a **waterslide** called the **Black Hole,** in which you ride through **complete darkness.**

8 IMG Worlds of Adventure in Dubai, United Arab Emirates, is the **world's largest indoor amusement park** spanning 1.5 million square feet (139,355 sq m).

9 The **Insanity** is a ride that **dangles you** above Las Vegas, Nevada, U.S.A., spinning at **40 miles an hour** (64 km/h).

10 Holiday World & Splashin' Safari in Indiana, U.S.A., is home to the **world's longest water coaster,** measuring at 1,763 feet (537 m), which is over **three times longer** than the Washington Monument is tall!

1 The geographic cone snail **shoots venom** from a **harpoon-like** structure on the end of its nose.

2 Travelers are banned from **Snake Island** in Brazil because it's **home to** golden lancehead vipers, whose venom can **melt human flesh.**

3 Some hunters in the rainforest use **poison dart frog** **toxins** on their **blow darts.**

4 The bombardier beetle can **shoot hot poison** **from its rear end** 500 times a second.

5 The wood tiger moth is the **first species known** to secrete **nasty fluids** from a specific body part depending on the predator—from the **abdomen for ants,** from the **neck for birds.**

Alarming Facts About

Deadly Animals

6

The **tentacles** of the Portuguese man-of-war can be up to 165 feet (50 m) long.

7

The male **great bustard** bird impresses females by eating **blister beetles,** which contain a **poison** that rids the bird of parasites, helping it **look more attractive.**

8

The zombie worm **secretes acid** that is strong enough to **break down animal bone.**

9

The **blue-ringed octopus** is the size of a golf ball but carries venom **1,000 times** more powerful than cyanide.

10

The mouth of a wild **Komodo dragon** contains **powerful venom.** It will often bite its prey, tracking it until it **collapses.**

Music

Facts to Get Stuck in Your Head

1 The world's **smallest guitar** is only about the size of a human blood cell.

2 **Big Carl**—the nickname for the **world's largest tuba**—is eight feet (2.4 m) tall and needs three people to play it properly.

3 **Talking drums** were used in Africa for centuries to send messages over long distances.

4 The world record for **longest drum roll** is 12 hours, 5 minutes, and 7 seconds.

5 The **first saxophone** was made of wood, not brass.

8

Zookeepers at the Smithsonian National Zoo in Washington, D.C., gave one of their elephants instruments such as **harmonicas** and a horn to play, **using her trunk.**

10

A man from Germany set a world record for **cycling backward** while playing a violin: 37.6 miles (60.45 km) in 5 hours and 8 seconds.

7

One of the first **typewriters** was called a **"literary piano."**

9

The **Vegetable Orchestra** performs around the world on instruments made of **fresh vegetables,** like a pumpkin drum, carrot flutes, and a celery guitar.

6

Many musical instruments have made their way **into space,** including a keyboard, a guitar, and a **didgeridoo** (a wind instrument native to Australia).

Extreme Weirdness

BOATS GO SKIING

WHAT Snow kayaking

WHERE Otepää, Estonia

DETAILS Why sail on water when you can grab your boat and hit the slopes? Athletes at a ski resort raced in kayaks down a custom-made track of snow. Steering with their paddles, the racers glided over multiple snowbanks before finally crossing the finish line into a pool of water. Snow's up, dude!

GORILLA FOOLS HUMANS

WHAT Ape robot

WHERE Bristol, England

DETAILS Call it Planet of the Fake Apes. The Bristol Zoo Gardens' "Wow! Gorillas" exhibit featured an animatronic ape and several five-foot (1.5-m)-tall fiberglass gorilla sculptures. The sculptures were later painted and decorated by local artists. What's next—papier-mâché penguins?

CHOCOLATE DRESS

WHAT Candy clothing

WHERE Edinburgh, Scotland

DETAILS How do you celebrate National Chocolate Week? By wearing an entire outfit made of the sweet stuff. A Scottish designer created this chocolate look for a fashion show celebrating the tasty treat. In addition to the 110-pound (50-kg) dress, the model wore a chocolate hat and fan. That's one sweet-looking getup.

PIG ON WHEELS

WHAT Pig-shaped race car

WHERE Medellín, Colombia

DETAILS Oink, oink—er, honk, honk! Better get out of the way of this racing pig. The homemade car was one of many wacky vehicles that took part in a car festival. Wonder what other fun farm animals this swine swooped past?

PIZZA BED

WHAT Pizza slice sleeping bag

WHERE Glen Mills, Pennsylvania, U.S.A.

DETAILS Do you dream about pizza? Well, now you can sleep in it! This cozy sleeping bag looks like a slice of pizza and comes with a choice of toppings that can be detached and used as cushions. Among the comfy add-ons are broccoli, olives, pepperoni, and mushrooms. Hold the sauce, please.

T. REX SCORES GOAL

WHAT Dinosaur disguise

WHERE Carson, California, U.S.A.

DETAILS Who knew dinosaurs loved sports? A person in a *T. rex* costume kicked around a soccer ball during a game between California's LA Galaxy and Washington's Seattle Sounders. The fake predator hit the field to promote a local museum. Sounds like a roaring good time!

1

To figure out the **outside temperature** (in degrees Fahrenheit) add 40 to **the number** of **chirps** **a cricket makes** in 14 seconds.

2

When **humans are cold,** our bodies start to **shiver** to help raise our **body temperature.**

3

You are made up of **70 percent water.** When your body loses **just one percent** you'll start to **feel thirsty.**

4

Your body **loses heat** 25 times **faster in water** than it does in the **outside air.**

5

From 1914 to 1916, explorer **Ernest Shackleton** and his crew **survived** after being **stranded in the Antarctic.**

Facts About Survival to Keep You Going

6 The diving bell spider can **live underwater** by creating a **bubble-like** web around itself—it needs to come up for air only **once a day!**

7 Tardigrades **can survive** for more than **100 years** **without water.**

8 A former park ranger in Virginia, U.S.A., holds the record for **surviving the most** **lightning** **strikes**—7!

9 Karakul, a type of **sheep, store extra fat in their tails** so they can **survive** harsh conditions.

10 You can **start a campfire** using **an orange.**

Stinky
Facts to
Sniff Out

1

A
skunk's spray
can cause nearby **predators** to **choke** and **become temporarily blind.**

2

The eastern **skunk cabbage** gives off a skunk-like smell to **attract flies** to pollinate it.

3

When an **Africanized honeybee** feels **threatened,** it **alerts its fellow bees** by releasing a scent that smells **like banana.**

4

The sea hare **sea slug** releases a **smelly, slimy, purple ink** that makes the slug **taste worse** to predators.

Scientists say that **crested auklet** birds **smell like tangerines!**

6

A vanilla-scented goo that comes from a **beaver's behind** is sometimes used as a natural **food flavoring.**

5

Gingko tree seeds release a strong **vomit-like** smell to attract animals to eat them and **spread** the seeds.

8

7

Humans are considered one of the **smelliest mammals** because they release odors from nearly **every part** of their **bodies.**

9

The **citronella ant** emits a **lemony odor** to defend itself.

10

Hyenas produce a scent from their rear ends that they use to **communicate** with one another.

Weird Facts About Wild Animals

1 The babirusa is known as a **"pig-deer"**—it needs to **grind down** its tusks, otherwise they will grow back **into its skull.**

2 The white yeti crab is covered in a fluffy **furlike coat** that **helps the crab** find food in the deep sea.

3 When the southern right whale **swims,** it constantly **leaps out** of **the water.**

4 With a tiny head and a **long neck** for reaching branches, the gerenuk antelope is known as the **"giraffe gazelle"!**

5 Snub-nosed monkeys have an **upturned nose** that tends to **collect water—** the primates often **sneeze** to clear their **"nose puddles."**

6 The **dementor wasp,** named after creatures from the **Harry Potter** series, **injects venom** into cockroaches that makes them slow and **zombie-like.**

7
The tanuki, or "raccoon dog," looks like a **fluffy raccoon** but is more closely **related to a wolf.**

8
The flattie spider **doesn't make a web** and instead **spins around** on one of its eight legs to **snatch its prey.**

9
The Sunda **flying lemur** isn't actually **a lemur** and it **can't fly.** However, it can cover more than 328 feet (100 m) **in a single glide!**

10
The **tusk of a narwhal** is **actually a tooth** that can grow up to approximately **nine feet** (2.7 m) long.

Birthday

Facts That Take the Cake

1

The record for the **most expensive** birthday cake = $75 million!

2

One of the three songs sung most often in the English language is **"Happy Birthday to You."**

4

In Italy, people **tug on the earlobes** of the lucky birthday boy or girl to wish them good luck.

6

Piñatas in Mexico are often **filled with fruit,** not just candy.

5

Instead of celebrating *individual birthdays,* people from Vietnam typically celebrate **all birthdays** on **New Year's Day.**

7

It's tradition in Jamaica **to throw flour** at the birthday boy or girl, sometimes **soaking the person** with water first so the **flour sticks better!**

3

The Smithsonian National Zoo celebrated a young **panda's birthday** with a **frozen "cake"** made mostly of juices, fruits, and veggies.

8

Instead of a traditional birthday cake, Danish children receive a **"cakeman,"** and the birthday child **takes the head.**

Turn the page for more fantastic birthday facts!

13

In New Zealand, people **skip cakes** altogether and instead **enjoy sprinkles on top of toast,** called **"fairy bread."**

10

Eating a plate of **long noodles** is a Chinese birthday tradition that symbolizes living a **long life.**

9

The record for **the most lit candles** on a cake at one time was **72,585.**

11

Sprinkles are called **"hundreds and thousands"** in **Australia.**

12

The melody of **"Happy Birthday to You"** was written in 1893 by **two sisters** from Kentucky, U.S.A.

16

It's tradition in some Canadian provinces to **smear butter** on the birthday boy or girl's nose.

17

The term **"birthday cake"** was first used in **1785.**

20

In Russia, **birthday wishes** are usually carved into a **fruit pie crust.**

15

11 = The record for the number of candles lit by **someone's feet** in one minute!

18

November 26 is **National Cake Day** in the United States.

14

In the 1800s, during the Victorian era, **parents used their children's birthday parties to teach them manners.**

19

In the U.S., the third Monday of February—**Presidents' Day**—was originally called Washington's Birthday in honor of **George Washington.**

Fast Facts About Wild Rides

1

Formula 1 race cars could theoretically drive **upside down** at superhigh speeds.

2

Researchers are trying to develop a car tire made from **dandelions**.

3
The **temperature** inside a speeding race car can soar **up to 140°F** (60°C).

4
The first **electric cars** were invented in the 1830s.

5
In theory, it would take five to **six months** to **drive to the moon in a car** going 60 miles an hour (96.6 km/h).

6
The **"telephone car"** has a **car horn** that sounds like a phone's **ringer**.

7
There's a car that **once traveled** more than **200 miles** (322 km) powered only **by coffee.**

8
Only about **12 to 30 percent of the energy** from the fuel in a car **actually moves** the vehicle down the road.

9
The first **self-propelled** vehicle was invented by a French engineer in 1769 and was **powered by steam.**

10
The steering wheel of a Formula 1 race car has **more than 35 buttons, levers, lights, dials, and switches.**

Funky Facts About Fruits and Veggies

Bananas are considered **berries.**

2 The **city of Chicago,** Illinois, U.S.A., was **named after** the Native American word *chicagoua,* for a type of **garlic plant.**

1

3 **Cathead, Winter Banana,** and **Captain Kidd** are all names of **apples!**

4 At the local **Watermelon Thump Festival** in Luling, Texas, U.S.A., locals compete in a **seed-spitting** contest.

Lettuce and leafy greens were the first foods **grown in space.** **5**

Consistently consuming a **large** quantity of carrots, **6** say three large carrots a day, can **turn your skin yellow-orange.**

7

Chili peppers are actually **fruits.**

8

The **black sapote fruit looks like** an **overripe green tomato** on the outside, but looks and **tastes like chocolate pudding** on the inside.

9

The original **nickname for eggplant** in Europe was **"crazy apple."**

10

The **durian fruit,** found in Asia, is so **notoriously stinky** that it's **banned** from Singapore's trains.

1 Some say you can still **hear the banjo** twangs of a **former prisoner** at the famous **Alcatraz prison** in California, U.S.A.

2 People have claimed to see a **floating vampire** at Highgate Cemetery in England.

3 Former U.S. president William Howard Taft was reportedly **haunted** by the ghost of a **15-year-old** boy in the **White House.**

4 You can go on a tour to visit an **underground ghost town** called Mary King's Close that is said to be one of **Scotland's most haunted** places.

5 At the Stanley Hotel in Colorado, U.S.A., you might hear the **ghosts of children laughing** or the ghost of Mrs. Stanley **playing the piano.**

6 In York, England, a ghost named **Mad Alice** laughs as people walk by, and the ghost of **the Grey Lady** will **tickle the necks** of tourists at the Georgian Theatre Royal.

7 Poveglia Island, Italy, is considered to be **so haunted** that the government **no longer** allows **access to the public.**

8 At an **old fort** in New York, U.S.A., legend says a **headless soldier** has been seen emerging **from a well** at midnight.

9 If you want to **take a photo** of Robert, a supposedly **haunted doll** on display at a Florida, U.S.A. museum, you need to politely **ask his permission.** If he **tilts his head,** that means yes!

10 A cemetery on the island of Barbados claims that **its coffins** have mysteriously **moved by themselves.**

Spooky
Facts About
Haunted
Places

1

People can **celebrate all things garlic** at the annual garlic festival in California, U.S.A., including **garlic ice cream.**

2

Proud Corgi owners bring hundreds of corgis to **Corgi Beach Day** in California where the dogs can **frolic** among thousands of bacon- and chicken-flavored **bubbles!**

3

Chase a **nine-pound** (4-kg) **wheel of cheese down a hill** in the U.K. at the annual Cheese-Rolling event.

4

In honor of a savory food called Yorkshire pudding, people **race down rivers in boats** made of flour, egg, and water in the U.K.

5

The **Bun Scrambling** Competition in Hong Kong invites competitors to **climb a tall tower** covered **in buns and collect** as many as they can in three **minutes!**

Facts About Fun

Festivals

to Celebrate

9 Every year, about **22,000 people** join the world's largest **tomato fight** in Spain.

10 If you aren't competing in the **Air Guitar World Championships**, you can still attend and take air guitar workshops with air guitar champions.

8 **Coffin Races =** 70 teams dress in **spooky costumes**, racing coffins down the **main avenue** of Manitou Springs, Colorado, U.S.A.

6 The **Night of the Radishes** = An annual event in which people compete by **carving intricate shapes into radishes.**

7 The three-day **Battle of the Oranges** takes place annually in Italy when teams adorned in armor storm the street hurling oranges at each other.

1 According to local legend, a **boy and a girl** with **green skin** arrived in Woolpit, England, in the 12th century and claimed to come from **another world.**

2 Taos Hum is a **strange buzzing noise** in the town of Taos, New Mexico, U.S.A.—**no one knows** where the sound is **coming from.**

3 A scientist once received a **72-second signal** from the constellation Sagittarius, and **who or what** the signal came from is **still unclear.**

4 In 1947, a **balloon crashed** at a ranch in Roswell, New Mexico, but many believe it was **actually a UFO** that the government tried to **cover up.**

5 In 1912, a man named Wilfrid Voynich purchased a **mysterious medieval book** that was written in a **language** and alphabet that **no one can translate.**

6 A farmer once claimed to have seen a **whole Bigfoot family** running through his ranch **carrying a pig.**

Puzzling
Facts About
Unsolved
Mysteries

7

King Tut's death is still a mystery— theories include everything from a **chariot crash** to malaria, or even being **bitten by a hippo!**

8

There have been more than **1,000 recorded sightings** of the **Loch Ness monster.**

9

Thousands of people have **observed mysterious balls of light** that float just **above the ground** near the village of Hessdalen, Norway.

10

Easter Island is covered in 900 **giant stone figures,** but no one knows for sure **who built them** or why.

KANGAROO VS. WALLABY

Kangaroos and wallabies are both marsupials, carrying their adorable young in their comfy, cozy pouches. But there are some major characteristics that set these two hind-legged hoppers apart. The most distinct difference is their size! Wallabies have much shorter hind legs, and they grow to be anywhere from roughly one to two feet (30 cm to 61 cm) tall, whereas kangaroos are much larger, sizing up to a height between three and eight feet (1 to 2.4 m) tall. Their size has a great deal to do with the different habitats they live in—kangaroos have longer legs to help them move quickly through open terrain; wallabies have shorter legs to help them be more agile in more wooded areas. These habitats also inspire their eating habits—kangaroos eat mostly grass, whereas wallabies munch on a variety of both grasses and plants.

What's the Difference?

Check out these similar pairings and see how you can determine this from that!

BANANA VS. PLANTAIN

These slender, delicious fruits both change colors, as well as flavor, at different stages of ripeness, but why would someone choose to eat a banana over a plantain or vice versa? Plantains are often cooked before they are eaten because eating one raw can be tough. They have less sugar and are a little starchier than bananas, giving them a more savory, dry texture. Because of this, they are often paired with other savory foods, like onions, whereas bananas tend to be paired with sweeter foods like yogurt or cereal, or set aflame in brown sugar for bananas foster. Bananas are much moister, making them easier to eat without being cooked.

RACQUETBALL VS. SQUASH

Both involve hitting a ball fast and wild in a fairly small enclosed room using some kind of racquet (racquetball) or racket (squash), but that might be as far as it goes for similarities when it comes to these two swatting sports! Racquetball started in America; squash began much earlier in England. In squash, the racket and ball are smaller than those in racquetball. But in racquetball the ball is much lighter, giving it a higher bounce and making for a fast-paced game, especially when there are practically no boundary lines and any surface can be used to bounce the ball off of, including the ceiling! In comparison, squash does have boundary lines, so no ceiling bouncing allowed. Thank goodness it does have boundaries, because with a heavier ball there is less bounce time, meaning a player needs to get to the ball quickly before it bounces again!

WEATHER VS. CLIMATE

What's the difference between weather and climate? Time! Weather generally refers to shorter periods of certain conditions. It might be sunny or raining—even changing one minute to the next—or we might be anxiously watching the news to see if schools will have a snow day! On the other hand, climate refers to the patterns that affect a particular area over a long period of time, given the average weather a specific region might see. For instance, Florida, U.S.A., is more prone to consistent, hot, humid weather and hurricanes, whereas Colorado, U.S.A., is more prone to dry weather, different seasons, and wildfires.

ENVY VS. JEALOUSY

These two words have confounded the laws of language since the 13th century! Depending on who you ask, there isn't much of a difference and they are often used interchangeably, but there are a few instances when it might be better to choose one word over the other. "Envy" tends to be used more often when someone lacks something that someone else has, whether looks, prized possessions, or even a certain stature in life. "Jealousy," on the other hand, usually refers to an emotion someone feels when something he or she already possesses is threatened; jealousy often comes into play in friendships and relationships.

CRICKET VS. GRASSHOPPER

These leaping, singing creatures are full of small and big differences that aren't always clear unless you're paying close attention. Crickets and grasshoppers both have antennae, but the cricket's are long, while the grasshopper's are short. But don't mistake their antennae for "ears," as they don't help them hear! A grasshopper's "ears" are in their abdomen, whereas crickets have them in their front legs. Both crickets and grasshoppers stridulate, which produces the cool music you hear coming from crickets that rub their wings together or grasshoppers when they rub their legs together. It's unlikely you'll hear their sweet tunes battling against one another, as grasshoppers usually play during the day and crickets at night.

129

Tricky Facts About Magicians

1 The **Merlin Award** is an award given to the **best magician** of the year from around the world.

2 Houdini's most famous trick was making an **elephant "disappear"** in a box by hiding it **behind a mirror** that reflected the **empty space** of the box, making the box appear empty.

3 Project Magic is a program that teaches **people with disabilities** how to **do magic tricks** to enhance **motor skills** and gain self-confidence.

4 The **Bullet Catch** is a magic trick in which a **gun is fired** at a magician who must **"catch" the bullet** with his or her mouth, hand, or other object.

5 Magician David Blaine trapped his **entire body in ice** for **63 hours,** 42 minutes, and 15 seconds on a busy street in **New York City.**

6

Muhammad Ali
wasn't just one of the **greatest boxers** of all time— he also **did magic tricks.**

7

Magicians
sometimes **spend years** perfecting one magic trick.

8

Jasper Maskelyne was a magician who helped **fight the Nazis** in WWII by **hiding tools and maps** inside everyday objects like **playing cards.**

9

Magicians must take a **magician's oath** to **protect the secrets** of the trade before another magician **teaches them** their tricks.

10

Charles, **Prince of Wales,** is a **member** of the "Magic Circle," an exclusive **club for magicians.**

Extreme
Facts About
Adventures

1

A Zorb is a giant **plastic ball** that a human can get inside of to **roll down a hill, float on water,** or even **play football.**

2

More than **400 people** worldwide have climbed the **Seven Summits,** which involves reaching the **highest mountain peak** on each continent.

3

As a popular pastime in India, people have **combined the sports** of limbo and roller skating into **"limbo skating,"** which is sometimes done **under cars!**

4

Extreme ironing is when people **iron clothes** in **weird situations,** including ironing while **skydiving** and ironing while **kayaking** rapids.

5

The first person to **walk on a tightrope** over **Niagara Falls** walked 1,300 feet (396 m). He then went back across **performing stunts.**

6

An Italian man **set the record** for the **deepest cycling** underwater at 218 feet, 11 inches (66.5 m).

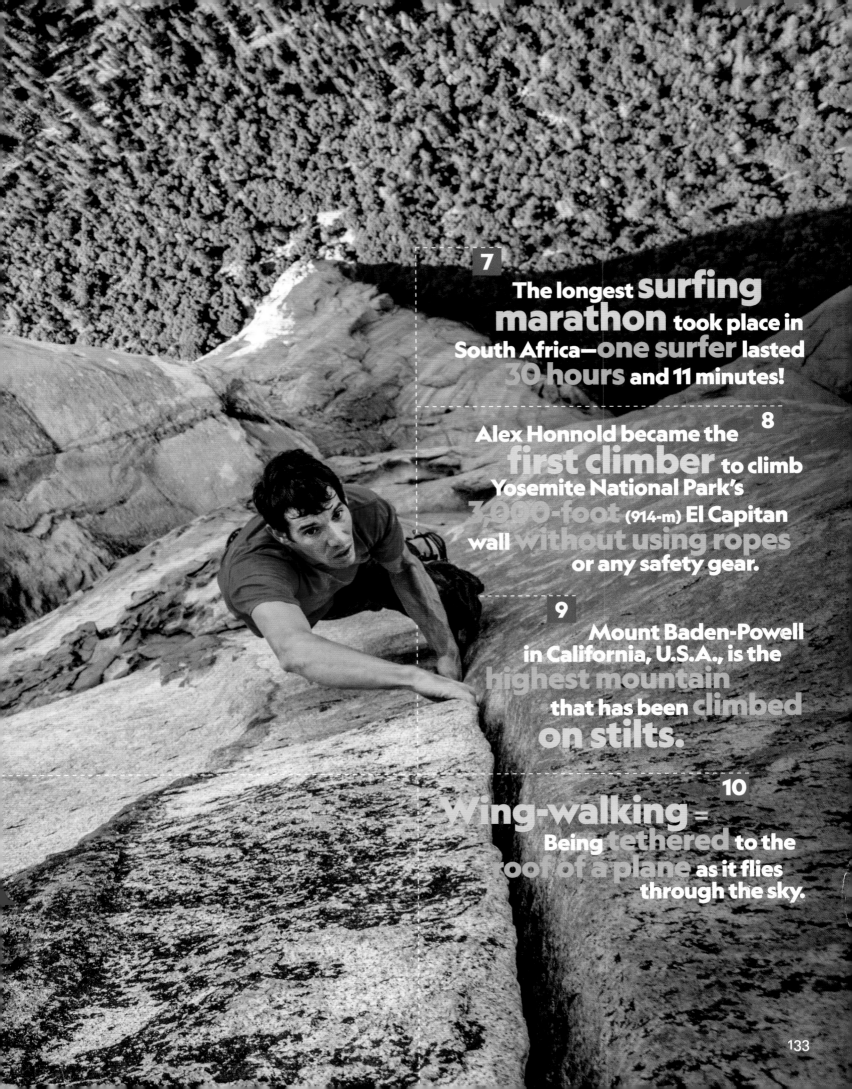

7

The longest **surfing marathon** took place in South Africa—**one surfer** lasted 30 hours and 11 minutes!

8

Alex Honnold became the **first climber** to climb Yosemite National Park's 3,000-foot (914-m) El Capitan wall **without using ropes** or any safety gear.

9

Mount Baden-Powell in California, U.S.A., is the **highest mountain** that has been **climbed on stilts.**

10

Wing-walking = Being **tethered** to the **roof of a plane** as it flies through the sky.

Shhh!... Secret Facts About Spies

1

Spies have used **weapons disguised as lipstick and pipes!**

2

In the 1960s, the CIA, the U.S. spy agency, provided **travel disguise kits** to spies.

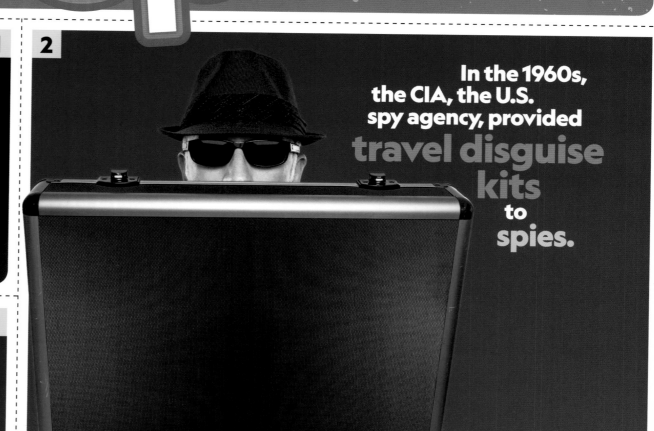

3

A real-life spy known as **"the limping lady"** had a prosthetic leg that she hid documents in.

4

Secret maps used to help spies escape to safety were hidden in **playing cards** in which the top layer of the card could be **peeled away** after being soaked in water.

5 Spies sometimes **passed messages** by leaving them inside a **dead rat** covered in **hot sauce** on the street—the hot sauce helped **scare away** any animals that tried to eat it.

6 The CIA issued **radio transmitters** camouflaged as pieces of **dog poop.**

8 The first **insect-size aerial vehicle** created to spy on the enemy looked like a **dragonfly.**

7 **Cameras** used to be **hidden** in many items, like **ties, shoes, walking sticks, pens, wallets,** and **handbags.**

T931759

9 A modified **makeup compact** was used to help **decipher codes** in mirrors.

10 During WWI, **cameras** were **strapped to pigeons** to capture pictures of **enemy weapons** and to **help create battle maps.**

Glowing

Jellyfish

Facts About

1 There is evidence that jellyfish lived in the ancient world at least 400 million years before dinosaurs existed!

2 Some types of jellyfish will eat peanut butter.

3 The lion's mane jellyfish can grow more than **100 feet** (30.5 m) **long** and up to seven feet (2 m) wide, rivaling the size of the blue whale.

8 Scientists have been **extracting a protein from jellyfish to power nanobots** (teeny tiny robots)!

10 One species of jellyfish is nicknamed **"pink meanie"** due to its intense sting and deep color.

5 Jellyfish **aren't fish—** they're actually **related to coral!**

7 A jellyfish's **tentacles** can still sting even when they break apart from the jellyfish's body.

9 Many jellyfish are considered **"Medusa"** jellyfish, which refers to a monster from Greek mythology with **wild snakes** for hair.

4 Jellyfish are made of more **than 95 percent water.**

6 Not only does the gooey, soft body of a jellyfish not contain **a single bone,** but it also doesn't have a head, a heart, a brain, eyes, ears, or a nose!

Funny Facts
to Keep You
Giggling

1 The sound of **your** **laugh changes** depending on **whether you're** chuckling **with pals** **or strangers.**

2 Between 10 and 15 minutes of **laughing burns** between **10 and 40 calories.**

3 **Laughter** reduces **stress.**

4 **Gelotology** = The **scientific study** of **laughter** and its effects on the body.

5 **Laughing** at a joke requires activity in **five different areas** of **the brain.**

6 **Apes and rats** appear to laugh **when tickled.**

7 **Laughter** can **strengthen friendships.**

8 There was an **outbreak** of **contagious laughter** in an African town that lasted for **several months** straight.

9 You're 30 times more **likely to laugh** when you're around **friends** than when **you're alone.**

10 Before humans used **spoken language,** some scientists believe they **used laughter** to **communicate** with each other.

1

The three-inch (8-cm) ruby-throated **hummingbird** can flap its wings up to **200 times** per second when **impressing a mate.**

2

Bumblebee bats weigh around **.07 ounce** (2 g)—that's only slightly more than an **index card!**

3

The Japanese **dwarf flying squirrel** hangs **upside down** on a branch while eating.

4

Because of their small stature, **mini horses** are used for a variety of **therapy** outlets, visiting more than **25,000 people** each year.

5

Pygmy hippos are **half as tall** as regular hippos.

6

A **tiny mite** the size of a sesame seed is the **fastest animal** on the planet.

7

Acmella nana is the world's **tiniest snail**, with a shiny, **see-through shell** that measures just .027 inch (.07 cm) tall.

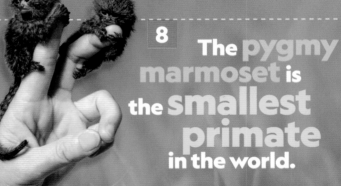

8

The **pygmy marmoset** is the **smallest primate** in the world.

9

The record for the **smallest horse** is **17 inches** (43 cm) tall to the withers (shoulder blades).

10

Pygmy hedgehogs are **lactose intolerant—**no cheese, please!

Itty-Bitty Facts About Tiny Animals

Pygmy hedgehog

A Gallery
of Amusing Facts About
Museums

1 The Museum of **Bad Art** has an **entire section** dedicated to paintings with **blue people** in them.

2 The Cancún **Underwater Museum** in Mexico has 500 **life-size structures** underwater that people can visit by **glass-bottom boat, snorkeling,** or **scuba diving.**

3 The Vent Haven Museum in Kentucky, U.S.A., houses **hundreds** of **ventriloquist dummies.**

4 The International **Cryptozoology** Museum in Maine, U.S.A., claims to have **poop samples** from **Bigfoot.**

The **Lunchbox Museum** in Georgia, U.S.A., has **more than 2,000** lunch boxes.

5

The Sulabh International **Museum of Toilets** in India traces the **4,500-year history** of the toilet, and it even has a toilet that **looks like a bookcase** on display.

6

The **Salt and Pepper** Shaker Museum in Tennessee, U.S.A., boasts **over 20,000 pairs of shakers.**

8

7

There is a **lawn mower** museum in Great Britain where you can view **lawn mowers** of the **rich and famous.**

9

Head to the **Mütter Museum** in Philadelphia, Pennsylvania, U.S.A., to see a piece of **Albert Einstein's** brain.

10

The **Mustard Museum** in **5,992 jars** Wisconsin, U.S.A., has of mustard on display from 70 countries, plus a mustard **vending machine.**

Mountain Majesty Comes in Many Shades

Rainbow-colored foothills stretch for miles, their bright ridges popping against the blue sky. Boasting red, gold, orange, yellow, and blue stripes, the slopes look as if they belong in a sci-fi movie. But these formations are real, located right here on planet Earth. Part of Zhangye Danxia National Geopark in north-central China, the all-natural rock rainbows took millions of years—and a lot of shaking, rattling, and rolling—to form.

LASTING LAYERS

The hills of Zhangye Danxia (pronounced JANyeah DAN-siah) are nestled in a basin against the Qilian Mountains in China's Gansu Province. Covering about a hundred square miles (259 sq km), the slopes are hundreds of feet tall. Many have several stripes of color. How did these hills get their painted look? This landscape is made of layers of rock called strata. Similar to a tiered cake, it was created one layer at a time. The first sheet formed some 24 million years ago. Wind and water eroded parts of the land surrounding the basin, grinding it into sediment (or bits of rock). The pieces settled across the basin floor like a thick blanket, and eventually the sediment hardened. Over time, changes in climate affected the rate of erosion and appearance of the sediment that was produced from rocks surrounding the basin. Each new erosion phase brought a new color of sediment into the basin, in time creating another sheet of rock on top of the old one. This process happened over and over again until the basin was covered with hundreds of layers.

Danxia means "rosy cloud" in Chinese.

Red layers of rock come from iron that has rusted.

The continent crash that made these slopes also made the Himalaya!

CRUNCH TIME

The colorful formations in the basin at Gansu may have remained hidden under its top layer if not for a geological event that was literally shaking up the whole region. It all started in Earth's lithosphere. This is the outer layer of the planet, which is divided into huge plates that are constantly moving. Sometimes the movement of the plates slowly pushes up land on the surface and eventually creates hills and mountains.

SMASHING STRIPES

About 50 million years ago, the plate that carries the country we now call India began to collide with the plate that holds the rest of Asia. The crash was so powerful that it pushed chunks of land just south of the spot where Zhangye Danxia is located. Here, jagged mounds of earth rose over millions of years, revealing the ground's multicolored stripes. (The land was tilted as it was forced upward, which is why the layers run diagonally rather than horizontally.) Weathering and erosion smoothed over the rugged rocks and formed the rounded hills that you can see now.

A COLORFUL DRAW

In 2011, the Chinese government declared Zhangye Danxia a national park. Thousands of people visit every year to check out one of nature's ultimate art projects. But the rocky spot isn't done changing. Natural forces such as erosion continue to slowly transform the landscape. So, in another 24 million years, the area may look totally different. You'll just need a time machine to actually see those changes!

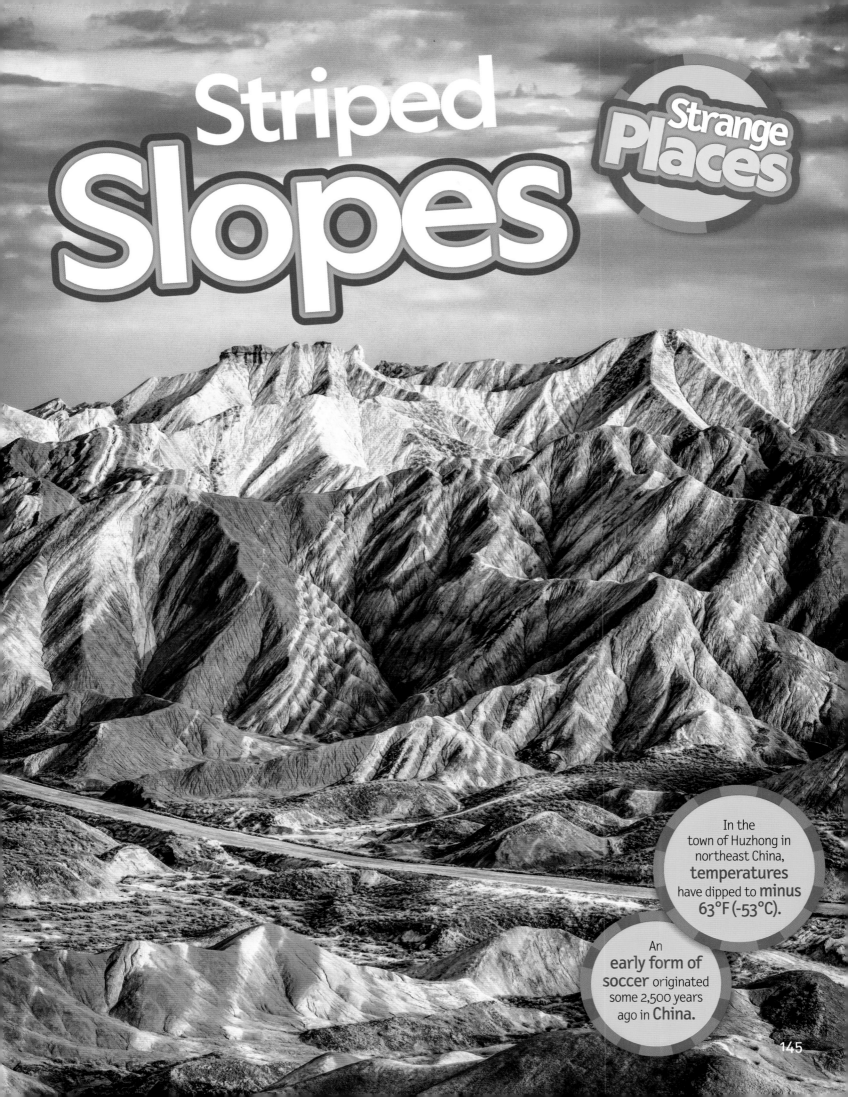

Striped Slopes

In the town of Huzhong in northeast China, **temperatures** have dipped to **minus 63°F (-53°C)**.

An **early form of soccer** originated some 2,500 years ago in **China**.

Bright Facts About
Biolumi

1 The bobtail squid has a specialized **light organ** that makes it seem **invisible** while it hunts.

2 The **U.S. Navy** monitors bioluminescence because some types of **algae** have been known to **endanger** military missions.

3 The **anglerfish** uses bioluminescence to attract its prey.

4 Bioluminescent Bay in Mosquito Bay, Puerto Rico, holds a **world record** for the **brightest** bioluminescent bay.

5 In Toyama Bay, Japan, the firefly squid creates **flashes of bright blue** that **people can see** between March and June.

nescence

6 The cookiecutter shark has a small glowing patch on its underbelly in the shape of a small fish to lure prey.

8 Most deep-sea bioluminescent creatures create blue or green light.

7 When the Atolla jellyfish is attacked, it sets off a light display called the "burglar alarm" that can be seen up to 300 feet (91 m) away!

9 For two weeks every May, a swarm of fireflies gather in the U.S.A.'s Great Smoky Mountains, putting on a "fireworks show."

10 In the Waitomo Caves in New Zealand, the walls twinkle with thousands of bioluminescent glowworms.

2

Alpaca moms **hum** to comfort their babies.

3

A **newborn** red kangaroo is 100,000 times **smaller** than its mother.

5

A newly hatched alligator rides on its mother's head or in her mouth.

1

Mzee, a **130-year-old** tortoise in Kenya, Africa, looked after Owen, a **baby hippo rescued** after he was washed out to sea by a tsunami.

4

A **baby fish** is called a **fry.**

7

Baby squirrels are called kits or **kittens.**

6

A **baby sloth** hangs from its mother's fur until it's about a year old.

Adorable
Facts About
Baby Animals

8 Baby birds learn their mother's song before they hatch.

9 Blue whale calves can gain up to 200 pounds (91 kg) a day in their first year.

10 Hedgehogs are born with soft spikes that take about three weeks to harden.

149

Fun Facts

to

Bear in Mind

1

Sloth bears can **close their nostrils** so that their mouth has **more power** to **suck bees** out of the hive, like a vacuum.

2

U.S. president Theodore Roosevelt had a **pet bear** while in office.

3

Polar bears have **black skin** under their fur.

4

Most bears do not **poop or pee** while they **hibernate.**

Kermode bear

5

The **kermode bear,** often called a **"spirit bear,"** is a rare species of a **black bear** that has **white fur.**

6

License plates are shaped like **polar bears** in Canada's Northwest Territories.

NORTHWEST TERRITORIES
2·992
CANADA   1983

7

A **mysterious chef** in San Diego, California, U.S.A., wears a **bear costume** while he **cooks** and hosts dinner parties in secret locations three times a week.

8

A bear helped **carry supplies** for the **Polish Army** in World War II.

9

All polar bears can trace their ancestry back to **one female brown bear** that lived over **20,000 years ago** in Ireland.

10

Sloth, sun, and spectacled bears do not hibernate.

Facts About Super Splurges

1 In 2005, the **original HOLLYWOOD sign** sold for **$450,400.**

2 A **robot** from a 1956 movie sold for **$5.3 million**, making it the most expensive **movie prop** ever sold!

3 A **bed** shaped like Cinderella's **pumpkin-turned-coach** starts at **$47,500.**

4 For **$2 million**, you can buy a **sports car** that can drive underwater.

Diamonds are a dog's best friend— you can buy a **$3.2-million dog collar** embedded with **1,600 diamonds.**

5

A grilled cheese sandwich once sold for **$28,000** online.

6

You can buy a gold-encrusted donut for $100.

8

9

A $1,770 hamburger at a London, England, restaurant **included caviar** sprinkled with **gold leaf.**

7

One lock of Elvis's hair sold for **$115,000.**

10

For nearly $7,000, you can buy a **dog bathtub** encrusted with more than **45,000 pink crystals.**

Action-Packed
Facts About
Sports

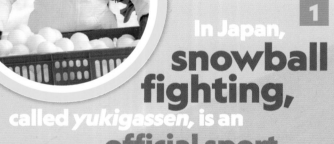

1 In Japan, **snowball fighting,** called *yukigassen,* is an official sport.

2 Pato, the national sport of Argentina, is a mix of **polo and basketball.**

3 Some daredevils cruise down **active volcanoes** on plywood boards.

4 Bikers in **scuba gear** pedal along the **Atlantic Ocean's floor** for an **annual race** off the coast of **North Carolina, U.S.A.**

5 Skyaking involves athletes **parachuting** from a plane while **strapped to a kayak** and then landing on water.

6 Winter waves off Cape Peninsula, South Africa, can **swell to 25 feet** (7.6 m), attracting daredevil **surfers.**

7 Abraham Lincoln was an accomplished **wrestler.**

8 The average **life span** of an NBA basketball is about **10,000 bounces.**

9 In the 1800s, baseball **umpires** sat in rocking chairs behind **home plate.**

10 Figure skating was once part of the **Summer Olympics.**

Relieving
Facts About Ridiculous
Restrooms

1
A **restroom stall** in Japan is built **inside an aquarium** where fish and sea turtles swim by as you **do your business.**

2
A **restroom** in Mexico has a transparent **glass floor** so that you can see the **15-story drop below.**

3
To **find the bathroom** at a restaurant in Milwaukee, Wisconsin, U.S.A., patrons must **navigate** through **mazes** and avoid a **trick door.**

4
You can find a **historic two-story outhouse** in a town in Illinois, U.S.A.

5

Astronauts on the International Space Station have to **strap down** their feet so they don't **float away** while **using the bathroom.**

6

Coca-Cola Park in Pennsylvania, U.S.A., has a **gaming system** in one of the restrooms.

7

There's a **restaurant** where guests **sit on toilet seats** and are served food on platters that look like **mini toilets.**

8

Australians celebrate **Australia Day** by racing "dunnies"—portable **toilets on wheels.**

9

Chongqing, China, is home to the **world's largest public bathroom—** the building has **1,000 toilets.**

10

You can **take a bath** surrounded by **elephants, giraffes,** and other **safari wildlife** at Madikwe Hills Lodge in South Africa.

BUS DOES PUSH-UPS

WHAT Exercising sculpture

WHERE London, England

DETAILS This bus will get you pumped! Called the London Booster, the "muscular" double-decker was built in honor of the 2012 Summer Olympics in London. To create the installation, an artist fitted a real bus from the 1950s with electrical arms that move up and down, push-up style. Who knew buses could be bodybuilders?

Extreme Weirdness

WEAR YOUR LAWN

WHAT Grass-covered flip-flops

WHERE New South Wales Coast, Australia

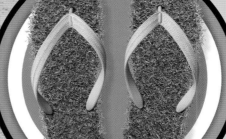

DETAILS Want to feel the grass between your toes? Just plant your feet in these grass-topped flip-flops, designed to give you the sensation of being outdoors anytime. Don't worry about watering the sandals—the grass is actually a layer of artificial turf. You'll have some happy feet!

ZIPPER OPENS APARTMENT

WHAT Unzipped floor

WHERE Tokyo, Japan

DETAILS You won't keep your lips zipped about this display! Built into the floor of an apartment, the temporary art installation is shaped like a giant zipper that's opening up the floor. The zipper is made of wood, so it doesn't actually move. But the artist hopes you'll look twice before zipping by.

BIIIGGG BINOCULARS

WHAT Binocular-shaped entrance

WHERE Venice, California, U.S.A.

DETAILS Did somebody ask for a better view? Sculptors Claes Oldenburg and Coosje van Bruggen designed this 45-foot (13.7-m)-tall set of binoculars that now serves as an office entrance for Google. So that's what they mean by "internet search."

GIANT SILVERWARE

WHAT Super-large spoon

WHERE Seoul, South Korea

DETAILS Think how much cereal could fit on this spoon. World Vision, a charity that works to end poverty, set up the spoon as part of an exhibit to collect donations for children in need. Giant coins were placed with the huge silverware to represent the money needed to help. Big spoon, big coins—and big hearts.

POTATOES ON PARADE

WHAT Spud-shaped tricycles

WHERE Lima, Peru

DETAILS Can you say spud-tacular? Potato sellers marched in a parade with potato-shaped carts for National Potato Day—a celebration of this food that originated in South America. This annual festival also includes a potato market and competitions to create the best potato-based dishes.

Heroic
Facts About
Daring Dudes

3 **Alexander the Great** was the king of Macedonia for 13 years and **never lost a battle** during his reign.

2 Shakespeare is known as the **greatest writer** of the English language and coined more than **1,700 words** that are still used today.

1 Robbie Maddison is a famous **motocross** star who did a backflip while **leaping over** the opened **Tower Bridge** in London, England, in 2009.

4 **Chief Sitting Bull** **stood up** to the U.S. government when it **attempted to take over** Lakota tribe land.

5

Charles Lindbergh was the first pilot to **fly nonstop across the Atlantic Ocean.**

6

Chesley "Sully" Sullenberger is a **pilot who safely landed a jetliner** carrying 155 people after the engine failed.

7

Harvey Milk helped pass a city ordinance in San Francisco, California, U.S.A., in 1978 that outlawed **discrimination** based on sexual orientation.

8

Bill Gates, the founder of **Microsoft,** donated $30 billion to form a foundation that works to **improve conditions** around the world.

9

Abraham Lincoln was president during the Civil War, during which he worked to keep the states together and helped **abolish slavery.**

10

Michael Jordan is considered the **world's greatest basketball player**—he led the Chicago Bulls to win six championships and took home five MVP awards.

Heroic

Facts About

Gutsy Gals

1

In 1979, Sylvia Earle took a walk 1,250 feet (381 m) below the surface of the **Pacific Ocean,** which set the record at the time for the **lowest depth** a human explored on foot.

2

Sabine Lisicki has the **fastest serve** in women's tennis, at 131 miles an hour!

(211 km/h)

3

For a long time, scientists believed that **humans were the only animals smart enough to create their own utensils for food,** but Jane Goodall discovered that **chimpanzees also use tools.**

4

Oprah Winfrey was born into **extreme poverty,** but she built a media empire worth **$4 billion** and is now one of the **richest people in the U.S.**

7

In 2015, **Misty Copeland** became the first African-American woman to be named a **principal dancer**—the highest level—in the 75-year history of the American Ballet Theatre.

9

First Lady **Eleanor Roosevelt** spoke up for those who didn't have a voice, and, at a time when few married women **had a career,** she matched the president's yearly income.

Ada Lovelace, a mathematician who lived during the 1800s, was the **first computer programmer.**

10

6

At the 1988 Olympics in South Korea, Jackie Joyner-Kersee **won three golds, a silver, and two bronzes**—and at the time held the most medals of any woman in **Olympic track and field** history.

8

Misty May-Treanor and Kerri Walsh Jennings **played volleyball** in **three different Olympics,** playing 43 sets and losing only one!

5

On June 18, 1983, Sally Ride became the **first American woman** and the youngest astronaut, at age 32, to **travel to space.**

What's the Difference?

CLUB SODA VS. SPARKLING MINERAL WATER

These bubbly beverages are exciting to drink, but why drink one instead of the other? Club soda doesn't have naturally occurring bubbles—the bubbles are added in by way of minerals added to the water! It doesn't have a very strong flavor, which makes it ideal for mixing with other liquids to create your own bubbly concoction. On the other hand, sparkling mineral water usually comes from a natural spring or well and is naturally carbonated. The minerals in sparkling water can make for a bitter or intense taste.

TSUNAMI VS. TIDAL WAVE

These terrifying beasts of water are actually created by different forces. Tidal waves often occur in shallow water when a high tide rises so rapidly that a "wave" develops. They are created by weather and gravitational forces from the sun or moon. Some tidal waves can be as tall as 50 feet (15.2 m), while tsunamis may reach up to 100 feet (30.5 m) high. Tsunamis usually consist of multiple waves, not just one, with waves sometimes being an hour apart. Unlike tidal waves, tsunamis are not formed by gravitational forces, but more by water displacement and disturbances from events such as earthquakes or even erupting underwater volcanoes.

LLAMA VS. ALPACA

Both of these fluffy, long-necked buddies hail from South America. Llamas are roughly double the size of their smaller alpaca counterparts. Their ears are different shapes and lengths as well, with the llama's ears much taller than the alpaca's short and stubby ones. But despite their differences in size, alpacas produce much more fibrous fur compared to llamas. Llamas have been bred as a pack-carrying animal for thousands of years, whereas alpacas have been bred for just as long but specifically for their luxurious fiber. Plus, llamas have actually been used to guard alpacas!

PAPAYA VS. MANGO

Their shape might be similar, but take one bite and you'll notice the differences immediately! The mango tends to be much sweeter and firmer than a papaya. You can tell a mango is ripe by the golden yellow color on the inside. Papayas, on the other hand, are much milder in taste, though still sweet, and considerably mushier. A ripe papaya is distinguished by its dark orange color. There are dozens of tiny seeds at the center of a papaya that can be eaten, but beware, they have a bit of a spicy flavor and are sometimes used as a pepper replacement. Mangoes, on the other hand, have one large seed in the middle.

HAIR VS. FUR

Only mammals have hair, and fur in particular is hair on nonhuman mammals. Sounds like it's just the word itself that's the difference, right? Not so much. Fur comes with its own benefits. For animals, fur provides them with protection from temperature, whether hot or cold, and can also protect them from rain. Hair on humans does not help regulate body temperature to nearly the same extent, if at all. Human hair can also continue to grow, and we simply cut it when we feel it gets too long, whereas animal fur tends to stop at a certain length and then fall out to be replaced.

Alpaca

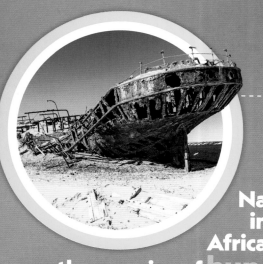

1 **Virgin Islands** National Park features a 225-yard (206-m)-long **underwater snorkeling trail!**

2 **Skeleton Coast** National Park in Namibia, Africa, is home to the remains of **hundreds** of **shipwrecks.**

3 **Wood Buffalo National Park** in Canada has the **world's largest beaver dam**—it's nearly **nine times** as long as the **Statue of Liberty** is tall.

4 The **oldest human remains** (2.8 million years old) were found in **Serengeti** National Park, Tanzania.

5 **Great Smoky Mountains** is the **most visited** national park in the **United States.**

6 The **Yarlung Tsangpo** Grand Canyon in the Himalaya is **17,000 feet** (5,300 m) **deep**—that's three times **deeper** than the U.S.A.'s **Grand Canyon.**

7 **Crater Lake,** in Oregon, U.S.A., is 1,943 feet (592 m) deep, enough to hide **1.5 Empire State Buildings.**

8 The **longest cave** system in the world is at **Mammoth Cave National Park,** Kentucky, U.S.A., where more than **405 miles** (652 km) have been explored.

9 The **Old Faithful** geyser at **Yellowstone National Park,** Wyoming, U.S.A., **can shoot** out of the ground **up to 184 feet** (56 m)

Canaima National Park, Venezuela, features the **world's tallest waterfall, Angel Falls.**

Facts About

National Parks

to Explore

Fierce Facts About Vikings

1
Viking boots were often made of goatskin.

2
A rare hoard of Viking treasure found in Scotland contained jewelry, armbands, brooches, and cross necklaces.

3
Vikings didn't wear horned helmets—that look was popularized by painters.

4
Distinguished Vikings were sometimes buried in ships that would be set on fire and pushed out to sea.

5
Vikings worshipped a god named Loki who could shape-shift into different animals.

6
Vikings enjoyed skiing and worshipped a skiing god named Ullr.

7
The name "Viking" means "a pirate raid" in Old Norse language.

8 Thursday is named after **Thor**, the Norse god of thunder.

9 Denmark is home to the Ladby ship, a **ship burial** of a Viking king that dates back to the year 925.

10 A group of Viking warriors called **berserkers** wore bear or wolf skins and howled in battle like wild animals.

Energetic Facts

About

Electricity

1

You're **more likely to get a shock** from **static electricity in winter than in summer.**

A platypus hunts using **electrical impulses.**

2

3

A Japanese **aquarium once used an eel to power the lights** on a Christmas tree.

4

The electricity in Albertville, France, is **powered by cheese.**

Only one percent of a **microwave's** time is used to heat food; the other 99 percent of the time it is in standby mode, using **more electricity** to **power its clock** than heating food.

5

6

There is a pedal-powered cinema in which a few people **pedal bicycles** to power an outdoor **movie theater** for up to 500 people.

Nearby lightning strikes can cause some **mushrooms** to multiply and **grow in size** in the wild.

7

8

The **Oriental hornet traps sunlight** in its "skin" and turns it into electricity.

9 **10**

Muscle cells in the heart contract due to electricity that runs **through your body.**

Sharks can **detect electric fields** thanks to the thousands of **tiny pores** on their heads that are **filled with** an electrically conductive jelly.

The Dumbo octopus

is known for its adorable elephant-like ears and is the world's deepest-living octopus species,

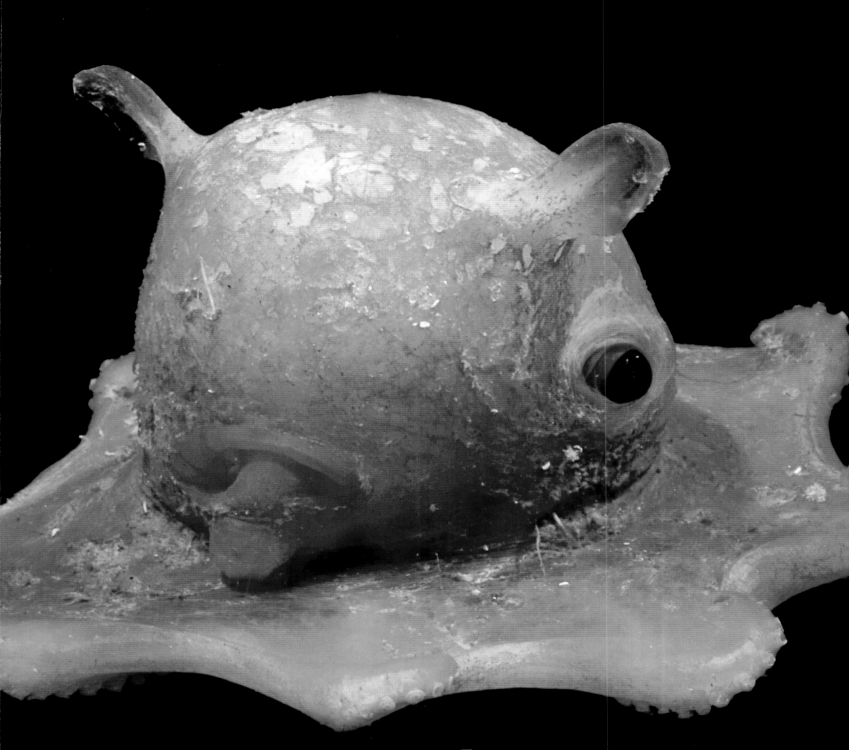

some living as deep as

23,000 feet (7,000 m)
below sea level.

Futuristic Facts About Technology

1

The **Int-Ball** is an **adorable drone,** slightly larger than a softball, **that floats** through space on its own or can be **remote-controlled from Earth.**

2

The **Weird Hotel in Japan is staffed almost** totally by **robots,** including a **dinosaur robot** receptionist that checks you in.

3

Dobi Robots broke a world record for the **largest number** of **robots dancing** at the same time: **1,069.**

4

Harry the robot knows **how to play the trumpet.**

A music-performing **band of robots** called Z-Machines has a guitarist with **78 fingers** and a drummer with **22 arms.**

5

Robear is a **robot nurse** with the face of a bear that helps care for patients by **lifting them** out of bed into a wheelchair.

6

Researchers study geckos to learn how to **help robots** and **astronauts** maneuver around space structures.

8

7

Russia once **built a computer** powered by **water.**

9

There is a **Rubik's Cube** robot that can **solve itself.**

10

The world's **largest walking robot** is a **dragon** measuring **51 feet 6 inches** (15.7 m) long and **26 feet 10 inches** (8.2 m) tall that can **blow flames.**

175

1
Like humans, monkeys do not **eat the skins** of **bananas;** they **peel them** open!

2
Monkeys **groom each other** not only to get rid of dirt and parasites, but also to show **affection** toward one another.

3
At Jigokudani Monkey Park in Japan, **snow monkeys** bathe in natural **hot springs** during the winter.

4
The howls of **howler monkeys** can be heard up to **three miles** (5 km) **away.**

5
You can tell **how healthy** a bald uakari is by the **shade of red** on its face.

6
Monkeys have tails, but apes do not.

7
Capuchin monkeys are often trained to **assist people** who have lost movement in their body to do **helpful tasks** like turning **light switches** on and off.

8
Brazil is home to more than **50 species** of monkeys—that's more than any other country in the world!

9
One man paid **$25,000** for a collection of **paintings** by a chimpanzee.

When the beloved children's book character **Curious George** debuted in the United Kingdom, **his name** was changed to **Zozo.**

Playful Facts to Monkey Around With

Amazing Facts About Roadside Attractions

1 Check out a giant **dragon statue** made completely out of **porcelain dishware** in Yangzhou, China!

2 The walls in **Bubblegum Alley** in California, U.S.A., are covered in **20 years'** worth of chewed gum.

3 You can **visit a house** in Headington, England, that has a sculpture on the roof of a **giant shark** diving into the attic.

4 The world's **smallest church** is in New York, U.S.A., in the middle of a pond.

5 Visit **Larry the Lobster** in Kingston South East, Australia, where he stands at **56 feet** (17 m) tall.

6 Riders can **wait for the bus** inside a **strawberry** or other **fruit-shaped bus stops** in Konagai, Japan.

7 There's a **watchtower** in Colorado, U.S.A., with a nearby gift shop **shaped like a UFO.**

8 There is a **Ouija board tombstone** in a cemetery in Maryland, U.S.A., for the man who **patented** the board.

9 Take a drive on the **Enchanted Highway** in North Dakota, U.S.A., where you can see sculptures of **giant grasshoppers.**

10 When it snows in Minneapolis, Minnesota, U.S.A., a massive sculpture of a **spoon and cherry** looks like the world's largest sundae.

Giraffes
and humans
have the same
number of bones
in their necks:

7.

Behind the Facts

We're sure you're wondering how we got so many awesome facts about so many awesome topics into this book. First, we came up with a list of all the coolest and most interesting things out there—things we know kids want to know more about. Like wild and wacky animals and strange things about space. Caves, chocolate, and birds. Amusement parks. Slime. Baby animals. All kinds of stuff. Then we found 10 or 20 of the most exciting and surprising facts about those topics to arrange on each page. We carefully researched each and every fact to make sure it's absolutely true ... then we packed it full of cool bonus content! Things like strange places, moments of extreme weirdness around the world, and a feature called "What's the Difference?" that will answer age-old questions like "What's the difference between a kangaroo and a wallaby?" And we designed the pages so colorfully that you'll never get bored looking at them and will love flipping to all your favorite parts. Bet you didn't know who worked to make this book! It took a group of writers, editors, photo editors, and designers— the greatest book team around!

Illustration Credits

Index

Published by National Geographic Partners, LLC. All rights reserved.
Reproduction of the whole or any part of the contents without written permission
from the publisher is prohibited.

Since 1888, the National Geographic Society has funded more than 12,000 research,
exploration, and preservation projects around the world. The Society receives
funds from National Geographic Partners, LLC, funded in part by your purchase.
A portion of the proceeds from this book supports this vital work. To learn more,
visit natgeo.com/info.

NATIONAL GEOGRAPHIC and Yellow Border Design are trademarks of the National
Geographic Society, used under license.

For more information, visit nationalgeographic.com, call 1-800-647-5463, or write to
the following address:

National Geographic Partners
1145 17th Street N.W.
Washington, D.C. 20036-4688 U.S.A.

Visit us online at nationalgeographic.com/books

For librarians and teachers: ngchildrensbooks.org

More for kids from National Geographic: natgeokids.com

National Geographic Kids magazine inspires children to explore their world with
fun yet educational articles on animals, science, nature, and more. Using fresh
storytelling and amazing photography, *Nat Geo Kids* shows kids ages 6 to 14 the
fascinating truth about the world—and why they should care.
kids.nationalgeographic.com/subscribe

For information about special discounts for bulk purchases, please contact
National Geographic Books Special Sales: specialsales@natgeo.com

For rights or permissions inquiries, please contact National Geographic Books
Subsidiary Rights: bookrights@natgeo.com

Designed by Chad Tomlinson

The publisher would like to thank everyone who made this book possible:
Michaela Weglinski, project editor; Kate Hale, executive editor; Kelly Hargrave and
Brittany Moya del Pino, writers; Callie Broaddus, senior designer; Lori Epstein,
director of photography; Alison O'Brien Muff, photo editor; Sally Abbey, managing
editor; Joan Gossett, editorial production manager; Sophie Massie, fact-checker;
and Anne LeongSon and Gus Tello, design production assistants.

Hardcover ISBN: 978-1-4263-3435-1
Reinforced library binding ISBN: 978-1-4263-3436-8

Printed in China
19/PPS/1